The Logic Model Guidebook

Better Strategies for Great Results

Lisa Wyatt Knowlton • Cynthia C. Phillips

Phillips Wyatt Knowlton, Inc.

Los Angeles • London • New Delhi • Singapore • Washington DC

For information:

SAGE Publications, Inc.
2455 Teller Road
Thousand Oaks, California 91320
E-mail: order@sagepub.com

SAGE Publications Ltd.
1 Oliver's Yard
55 City Road
London EC1Y 1SP
United Kingdom

SAGE Publications India Pvt. Ltd.
B 1/I 1 Mohan Cooperative
    Industrial Area
Mathura Road, New Delhi 110 044
India

SAGE Publications Asia-Pacific
    Pte. Ltd
33 Pekin Street #02-01
Far East Square
Singapore 048763

Printed in the United States of America.

Wyatt Knowlton, Lisa
The logic model guidebook : better strategies for great results / Lisa Wyatt Knowlton, Cynthia C. Phillip.
        p. cm.
Includes bibliographical references and index.
ISBN 978-1-4129-5864-6 (pbk.)
    1. Proposal writing for grants. 2. Logic. I. Phillips, Cynthia C. II. Title.
HG177.K56 2009
658.15′224—dc22   2008019317

This book is printed on acid-free paper.

08   09   10   11   12   10 9 8 7 6 5 4 3 2 1

Acquisitions Editor:	Vicki Knight
Associate Editor:	Sean Connelly
Editorial Assistant:	Lauren Habib
Production Editor:	Karen Wiley
Copy Editor:	Kristin Bergstad
Typesetter:	C&M Digitals (P) Ltd.
Proofreader:	Wendy Jo Dymond
Indexer:	Holly Day
Cover Designer:	Bryan Fishman
Marketing Manager:	Stephanie Adams

The
Logic Model
Guidebook

For Taylor, my earth angel.
I know you will soar.

For Courtney and Nicholas, my greatest lessons learned.
You have taught me much.

Contents

Preface   ix

Acknowledgments   xiii

CONSTRUCTION   1

1. Introducing Logic Models   3
  Basic Concepts
    Models and Modeling   4
    Logic Model Benefits   4
    Logic Models Defined   5
    Logic Model Uses   5
    Two Types: One Logic   5
    Historical Background   6
  Examples   7
    Theory of Change Model Example   7
    Program Logic Model Example   8
    Program Logic Model and Evaluation Design   8
    Logic: No Guarantees   10
    Models Begin With Results   12
    Logic Models and Effectiveness   12
  In Summary   14
  Learning Resources   14

2. Building and Improving Theory of Change Logic Models   17
  Building a Theory of Change Model   18
    Getting Started   18
    Preferences and Styles   18
    Evidence Based and Plausible   18
    The Big Picture   19
    Multiple Strategies and Results   20
    Realistic Models   21
    Knowledge and Assumptions   22
    Action Steps: Creating a Theory of Change Logic Model   23
  Improving Theory of Change Models   24
    Multiple Perspectives   24
    "Unpack" and Share Assumptions   25

Toggling   26

Promising Practices and Benchmarking   27

Nonlinear Theory of Change Models   28

Doing the "Right Work"   29

Tough Questions   30

In Summary   31

Learning Resources   31

3. Creating Program Logic Models   **35**

From Theory of Change to Program Models   35

Assumptions Matter   36

Key Elements of Program Logic Models   36

Nonlinear Program Logic Models   38

Hidden Assumptions and Dose   38

Building a Program Logic Model   39

Program Logic Model Example   39

From Strategy to Activities   41

Action Steps for a Program Logic Model   44

Creating Your Program Logic Model   44

Creating a Program Logic Model Together   45

In Summary   46

Learning Resources   46

4. Modeling: Improving Program Logic Models   **49**

Modeling and Effectiveness   50

Context Challenges   50

Common Pitfalls: Blind Spots and Myths   50

Logic, Scale, and Specificity   51

Politics, Persuasion, and Perception   52

A Learning Culture and External Review   53

Quality Techniques   53

Modeling   53

Testing Model Quality: SMART and FIT   55

A "Mark Up"   56

Quality Questions   58

A Quality Model   60

"Better" Decisions   60

In Summary   61

Learning Resources   62

APPLICATIONS   **65**

5. Logic Models for Evaluation Literacy   **67**

Getting More Out of Evaluation   67

Connecting Management With Measurement   67

Evaluation for Effectiveness   69

Evaluation Design Basics   70

	Where Consumers Add Value	70
	Where Logic Models Add Value	72
A Design Example		73
	Two Kinds of Learning	73
	Key Evaluation Questions	74
	Indicators	77
	Indicators and Alignment	82
Results Require Choices		83
	Performance Standards	83
	Quality Evaluation Designs	84
	A Quality Framework	85
In Summary		85
Learning Resources		86

6. Display and Meaning **89**

Variation and Learning		90
	Graphic Display	90
	Complexity and Meaning	90
	Content, Uses, and Creation	91
	Model Benefits	91
	Alternative Approaches	92
Selected Cases		92
	Case 1: Promoting Preschool Change	93
	Case 2: Australian Sustainable Living Program	100
	Case 3: Canadian Studentship Program	104
	Case 4: Collaborative Learning, Inquiry, and Practice	107
	Case 5: Diffusing Ideas and Technologies	110
	Case 6: Evaluation System Development	113
In Summary		118
Learning Resources		118

7. Exploring Archetypes **121**

The Blank Page Challenge		122
Archetypes and Learning		123
	Recipes for Change	123
	Value of Archetypes	124
	More Critical Thinking	124
Selected Archetype Examples		125
	Example 1: Federal Block Grants	125
	Example 2: Pathways Mapping Initiative (PMI)	128
	Example 3: Public Health	130
	Example 4: Organizational Effectiveness	135
In Summary		138
Learning Resources		139

Name Index	**143**
Subject Index	**145**
About the Authors	**149**

Preface

Most people understand the relationship between what they do and what they get—afterward. The yield of actions taken isn't puzzling in retrospect. Hindsight is always 20:20. Forethought is more difficult. For example, most people have been late to a meeting, driven too fast, and gotten a traffic ticket.

When getting to an important meeting is the intended result, there are many choices to make. Why were we distracted from leaving the house earlier? Which is the bigger risk—being late or two additional points on your license? Most of the time, people seek specific results and take actions toward them. They rely on careful thought, skillful implementation, and reliable feedback to navigate choices. This process raises common questions: *How do we pick the right work? How can we make better decisions? How do we increase our chances for superior results?*

As people and their work efforts seek particular outcomes, these questions apply to many circumstances. The questions reflect ubiquitous issues for organizations, initiatives, projects, and programs. They apply to all our "doing": manufacturing, education, health care, a range of social dilemmas, and even our personal, daily lives.

As both demanding learners and passionate professionals focused on change, we have used logic models with great success for more than a decade. We believe *enlightened* trial and error is smarter than just trial and error. We think we ought to use what is known. Logic models can be a tool in a disciplined process that helps learning about and achieving impact. We wrote *The Guidebook* for people, like us, who want to "get" great results. While not a perfect remedy, logic models and modeling represent an incremental innovation because *pre*testing and *re*testing can improve decisions, implementation, and adaptation. They can contribute to effectiveness.

This text provides the reader with a basic understanding of how to create and use logic models. It is designed for both practitioners and students. We expect it to be of use to those in the nonprofit, government, and private sectors where the responsibilities of program design, planning, managing, communication, and evaluation are routine.

We approach logic models as important thinking and inquiry tools, and logic modeling as a process that contributes to clarity about a sequence of interactive relationships. Logic models display relationships of many kinds: between resources and activities, activities and outcomes, outcomes and impact. This display provides an opportunity to review critically the logic of these relationships and their content. Are the underlying assumptions, choices, and relationships sensible, plausible, feasible, measurable? Logic models assist strategy and contribute to performance management through discovery of the most effective means to a specified result.

The model examples in this *Guidebook* have flaws. We think all models are "drafts." There are no perfect models. The nature of models as a representation of perception (even when grounded in knowledge) reflects choices that have consequent limitations. As individuals and groups have "blind spots," the models they create will contain them too. Even so, models and modeling offer a potent alternative to lengthy narrative because visual display provides some easy ways to create shared understanding and to test quality.

The modeling process includes a cycle of display, review, analysis, critique, and revision to improve the model. These actions steps, tackled with colleagues or stakeholders, can contribute significantly to more informed displays and, ultimately, more successful programs and projects. We believe a thorough understanding of models evolves from using them. Modeling ensures that through practice, skill evolves—particularly if others are invited to contribute to and participate in model improvement through constructive critique. Using logic models in a systematic and disciplined approach to design, planning, communication, and problem solving supports learning. The modeling dialogue contributes to a commonly held map leading to results.

Chapters in the *Guidebook* are intended to support readers' changes in awareness, knowledge, and skill. It has two parts: construction and applications. Chapters 1 through 4 help readers understand, create, and improve models. These chapters help in the construction and quality of logic models. Applications are explored in Chapters 5 through 7. These chapters tackle the use of logic models.

In all chapters, we provide an overview, learner objectives, questions, exercises, and further resources. We introduce logic models in Chapter 1. Chapters 2 and 3 describe two types of models: theory of change models and program logic models. These chapters explain elements of the models and support their construction. Chapter 4 describes improving models—which is critical in the evolution of your program or project because it can influence your intended results.

Chapters 5 through 7 help readers see and understand model use. The practical ways logic models can assist in monitoring and evaluation is the focus of Chapter 5. It is written to assist evaluation consumers. Chapter 6 provides cases of logic model use from an array of thoughtful contributors. These applications are provided to show both the range of use and their variation in display and content. Last, Chapter 7 displays some archetypes, or reliable evidence-based recipes, that we hope will help readers see how to get quickly beyond a blank page. The content of Chapters 5 through 7 is intended as a rich field for learning about existing models. These chapters demonstrate just a tiny sampling of how logic models generally contribute to a range of functions and disciplines.

We hope this text is read and used in ways that support better thinking, strategies, and models. Most important, we hope it contributes to your great results.

The Logic Model Guidebook:
Better Strategies for Great Results

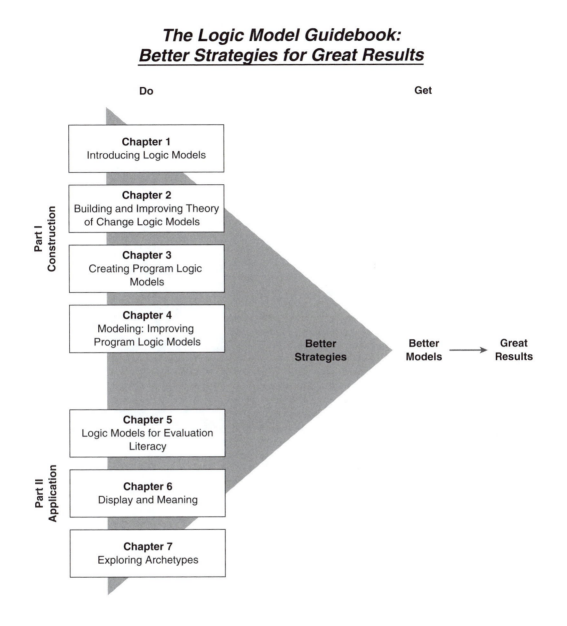

Acknowledgments

The *Guidebook* has benefited from the contributions of many people. Across the years, we have gained new insights and tremendous experiences because of our clients. Our first and warm thanks go to them.

In Chapter 6, there are six cases from generous collaborators who gracefully responded to our requests. We appreciate the time and effort these colleagues made to enrich the text. They include:

Case 1: Promoting Preschool Change—Gale Berkowitz, DrPH, Director of Evaluation; Kathleen Reich, MPP, Program Officer, Leader, Preschool Grantmaking; Lois Salisbury, JD, Director, Children, Families and Communities Program, The David and Lucile Packard Foundation. Julia Coffman provided the Kingdon models.

Case 2: Australian Sustainable Living Program—Sue C. Funnell, MA, Director, Program Improvement Pty. Ltd., New South Wales, Australia.

Case 3: Canadian Studentship Program—Gail V. Barrington, PhD, President, Barrington Research Group, Inc., Alberta, Canada; Mark Taylor, MSc, Director, Grants and Awards, Alberta Heritage Foundation for Medical Research; Richard Thornley, MLIS, MPH, Manager-Evaluation, Analysis and Information Services, Alberta Heritage Foundation for Medical Research.

Case 4: Collaborative Learning, Inquiry, and Practice—Beverly A. Parsons, PhD, Executive Director, InSites.

Case 5: Diffusing Ideas and Technologies—Gretchen B. Jordan, PhD, Principal Member of Technical Staff, Sandia National Laboratories, and John H. Reed, PhD, Principal and Owner, Innovologie.

Case 6: Evaluation System Development—Sherry Rockey, Vice President, Independent Sector.

Several other exceptionally capable professionals contributed to our understanding of model development and applications. Some of their work is included in Chapter 7. They include Astrid Hendricks, PhD, Michael Goodstadt, PhD, C.Psych., Barbara Kahan, Vicky Marchand, Jared Raynor, Lisbeth Schorr, and Peter York.

Our editor at Sage, Vicki Knight, has been helpful in countless ways. As new authors, we appreciate her wise guidance, delightful humor, and positive energy from start to finish. Thanks to Sage staff, Lauren Habib and Sean Connelly, for their talents and resourcefulness. A special nod also goes to Kristin Bergstad, our copyeditor. We learned a lot from her.

Several readers offered valuable critique and constructive feedback on all chapters. They include Kathryn Agard, EdD; John Bare; Tom Chapel; Richard Elmore, EdD; Janice Molnar, PhD; Lois-Ellen Datta; Faye Richardson-Green; Craig Russon, PhD; and Jim Sanders, PhD. Their comments were often provoking and always instructive.

Friends offer a special sort of encouragement on the journey of authorship. We are grateful to Kathryn Agard, EdD; David Dempsey; Sharon Dodson, PhD; Jim and Deana Draze, PhD; Cheryl Endres; Karen Gilbert; Steve Jessup; Eva and Jim Kendrick; Annette Luetzow, MD; Karen Vigmostad, PhD; and Marilyn Wiersma for cheering us on. We also appreciate the insights and stimulation of professional colleagues along the way, Drs. Zoe Barley, Paul Freddolino, John Gargani, Mark Jenness, Goldie MacDonald, Nancy Mansburger, Ricardo Millett, and Kathy Zurcher.

Finally, family provides important support in the challenges of creating a book. They were witness to the worry and long hours. In so many ways, their care and comfort sustained us. We thank and applaud, with love, Timothy Knowlton, Taylor Wyatt Knowlton, Meg Walton, Dennis Phillips, Courtney Phillips Long, and Nick Phillips.

PART I

Construction

CHAPTER 1

Introducing Logic Models

This chapter introduces logic models. There are two types: theory of change and program. This chapter describes model benefits and uses, and explains the role of modeling in both program and organizational effectiveness. Modeling begins with results, and quality models are evidence-based.

Learner Objectives

- Explain the difference between models and modeling
- Recognize the benefits and uses of logic models
- Demonstrate how to "read" a logic model
- Recognize types of models and their characteristics
- Describe the ways that models can support effectiveness

Most of us have had an assignment where we were required to get results. Perhaps you have been asked to design a new program, lead a change project, or plan an evaluation. Did drafting a narrative to circulate feel fragmented or inadequate? Did you think: "Where do I begin?" Logic models and modeling can be a potent option to resolve your dilemma. *The Guidebook* provides the practical support you need to create and use models. It will also enhance your understanding of the relationships between actions and results. Step by step, we describe logic models as both a tool and a process that resonates with learning and evidence-based design.

Basic Concepts

Models and Modeling

Logic models support design, planning, communication, evaluation, and learning. They are often used when explaining an idea, resolving a challenge, or assessing progress. They can untangle and clarify complex relationships among elements or parts.

Logic models are a graphic way to organize information and display thinking. They are a visual approach to the implicit maps we all carry in our minds about how the world does or *should* work. Logic models are tools that convey a scheme, program, or project in a brief, visual format. Logic models describe planned action and its expected results. A model is a snapshot of an individual's or group's current thinking about how their idea or program might work.

Modeling is a technique. The process of modeling encourages iterative development of an idea, program, or project. It can create a safe space to start a debate, generate ideas, support deliberations, and think more clearly about specific relationships. A single, coherent logic reflects a consistent thread that connects design, plans, execution, and evaluation. This thread of evidence-based logic is critical to program and organizational effectiveness.

Modeling allows careful consideration of the relationship between activities and results. When tackled by a team or small group of stakeholders, models can be improved by engaging the knowledge and experience of others. We think modeling is too frequently underutilized. We believe the best models are socially constructed in a shared experience that is facilitated. The shared understanding and meaning they produce among colleagues is valuable and enables success in subsequent steps of implementation and assessment.

Logic Model Benefits

In addition to extraordinary execution, organizational effectiveness ultimately requires design, planning, monitoring, and success measures. Logic models can contribute to the quality of all of these. In Chapters 1 through 4, we address models from the design and planning perspective. In Chapter 5, we offer more detail about their use with monitoring and evaluation. Logic models also:

- Offer highly participatory learning opportunities.
- Document explicit outcomes.
- Clarify knowledge about *what works* and *why.*

When logic models and modeling are used as a standard technique they can influence an organization's effectiveness. Logic models offer the strategic means to critically review and improve thinking. And better thinking always yields better results.

Effectiveness is not limited to—but certainly depends on—a clear vision, capable implementation, and the means to monitor both processes and results. Logic models can be a tremendous support for creating and communicating a common understanding of challenges, resources, and intended success. Moreover, models can also be used to calibrate alignment between the "big picture" and component parts. They can illustrate parts of or a whole system. For example, a logic model can display the learning objectives for an elementary Spanish curriculum or what a school district will do to secure student achievement.

Logic Models Defined

Logic models are a visual method of presenting an idea. They offer a way to describe and share an understanding of relationships among elements necessary to operate a program or change effort. Logic models describe a bounded project or initiative: both what is planned (the doing) and what results are expected (the getting). They provide a clear roadmap to a specified end. The development of models (or the modeling process) provides an opportunity to review the strength of connection between activities and outcomes. Through the experience of critical review and development, models can display participants' learning about what works under what conditions. Models are the product of modeling—which we believe is best done in small groups of stakeholders with the aid of intentional facilitation. They complement systems thinking as a tool and technique for achieving valid but simplified representations of real-world complexities. Common synonyms for logic models include idea maps, rich pictures, action maps, and mental models. Although logical frameworks (logframes) and causal loop diagrams (systems dynamics) are used for purposes similar to logic models, they are fundamentally different but complementary tools.

Logic Model Uses

While often used in the nonprofit sector among large nongovernmental organizations and foundations, logic models are of increasing interest among community-based organizations and the private sector, too. Because models enhance learning through the iterative exchange of information and experience, they offer important features to organizations that value evidence, diversity, dialogue, feedback, inquiry, great planning, and teams. Models can be used in program design, planning, implementation, and evaluation. For example, logic models can be used to design a marketing program, display a purchasing process, describe a school district's education improvement plan, create a community leadership program, or establish the best ways to resolve conflict.

Two Types: One Logic

We describe two types of models: theory of change and program. They differ by level of detail and use but represent the same logic. A *theory of change* model is simply a general representation of how you believe change will occur. A *program* logic model details resources, planned activities, and their outputs and outcomes over time that reflect intended results.

These two model types are different in their appearance and use. The level of detail and features distinguish theory of change and program logic models. Program logic models include more features than theory of change models. This concept of "view" is important and is discussed further in Chapter 4 because it influences the quality and utility of models. Theory of change models are conceptual, and program logic models are operational. Model types and their relative features are indicated in Table 1.1.

Table 1.1 Features of Model Types

Feature	Theory of Change Logic Model	Program Logic Model
Time frame	No time	Time bound
Level of detail	Low	High
Elements	Few ("do + get")	Many
Primary display	Graphics	Graphics + text
Focus	Generic	Targets + specified results

Relative to time frame, level of detail, volume of elements, display, and focus, the model types contrast. They are alike because they share the same research, theory, practice, and/or literature. Essentially, the types are different views of the same evidence-based logic that has a shared origin.

Model use differs in purpose(s). Theory of change models display an idea or program in its simplest form using limited information. These models offer a chance to test plausibility. They are the "elevator speech" or cocktail napkin outline of an idea or project. Program logic models vary in detail but offer additional information that assists design, planning, managing, and monitoring/evaluation. Program models support a display that can be tested for feasibility. They are the proposal version of an idea or project because they have fleshed out far more detail that often includes activities, resources, outputs, and other elements of interest to those creating and/or using the model.

Historical Background

Use of theory of change and program logic models began in the 1970s. Carol Weiss (1995), and Michael Fullan (2001) and Huey Chen (1994, 2005) are among the pioneers and champions for the use of program theory in program design and evaluation. U.S. Agency for International Development's (1971) logical framework approach and Claude Bennett's (1976) hierarchy of program effectiveness were among the earliest uses of the types of visual displays that have evolved into the program logic models we know today.

Logic models did not receive much recognition however until after the United Way of America came out with its publication *Measuring Program Outcomes* in 1996. This publication promoted the structures and vocabulary of logic models.

The W. K. Kellogg Foundation also was instrumental in spreading the use of logic models with its *Logic Model, Development Guide (2001)*. For those readers interested in more detail on the historical evolution of logic models, see the references provided at the end of this chapter.

Examples

In the examples that follow, we briefly explain the general concepts and terms related to a theory of change and to a program logic model. Chapters 2 and 3 provide more depth. Although we show one of each type of model, it is important to keep in mind that these are but two examples from a much broader continuum of possibilities. There are many ways to express or display the ideas and level of detail.

Theory of Change Model Example

Figure 1.1 shows a simple theory of change for leadership development. Read from left to right, it suggests some strategies, for example, curriculum and experiences, can positively influence people so they can more effectively tackle community challenges. This theory relies on the assumptions that training, experiential learning, and community orientation will have a substantial influence on individuals' skills and ultimately result in community development.

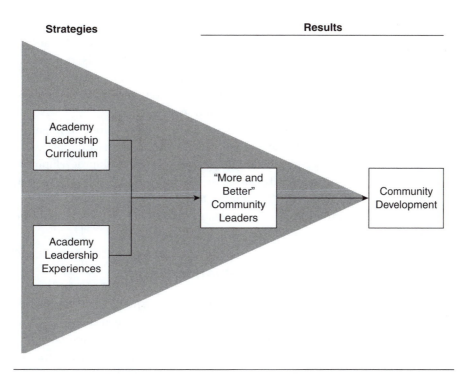

Figure 1.1   Community Leadership Academy Theory of Change

Chapter 2 focuses on creating theory of change logic models. They are the critical foundation for any change effort. Often, these models exist as part of an internal mental framework that is "dormant" or undisclosed. They can also imply considerable knowledge, experience, research, and practice. The evidence base for theory of change models typically is not made explicit.

Program Logic Model Example

Program logic models inventory, from start to finish, a specified program effort. For example, a program logic model for a community leadership program (based on the theory of change) would include the specified resources/inputs, activities, outputs, outcomes, and impact. Resources or inputs are what are needed to ensure the program can operate. Activities are the tactical actions (e.g., events, services, publications) that occur to fulfill the promise of each strategy. Together, activities make up the program design. Outputs are descriptive indicators of what the specific activities generate. Outcomes are changes in awareness, knowledge, skill, or behavior. The impact reflects changes over a longer period. Figure 1.2 displays a simple program model for the same community leadership program shown as a theory of change model in Figure 1.1.

This program model suggests desired results include more and better leaders and community development. It implies the leadership development agenda is about resolution of community challenges and that, if resolved, it contributes to community development.

To "read" this model, first note the intended impact (ultimate aim) of the program: community development. Then, move to the far left-hand side where resources or inputs essential to the program are listed. Logic models employ an "if–then" sequence among their elements. When applied to the elements in each column, it reads: *if* we have these resources, *then* we can provide these activities. *If* we pursue these activities, *then* we can produce these outputs. *If* we have these outputs, *then* we will secure these outcomes, and so on.

This model is *just one* very simple representation of how a program might be designed and planned for implementation. Many variations on this example could represent program design and planning for community leadership development that meets standards of logic and plausibility. We know that Figure 1.2, in fact, represents a program with some definite flaws. More discussion about how the program could be improved through a "mark up" (or critical review) that tests the program design is described in Chapter 4.

Program Logic Model and Evaluation Design

This guidebook also offers some support for using logic models to assist in evaluation design. This book will address only the framing of broad inquiry. At this level, evaluation questions are the foundation for evaluation design and planning. If we apply this to the community leadership program example, it is appropriate to focus on the program's intended results. The summative evaluation question is: What difference did the program make in the community's development? Perhaps

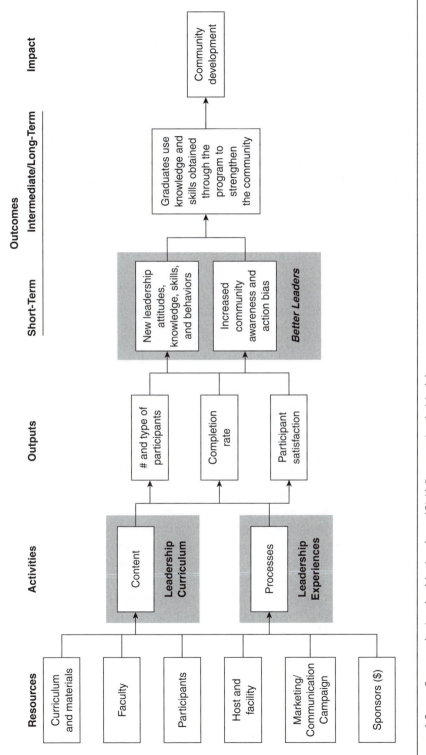

Figure 1.2 Community Leadership Academy (CLA) Program Logic Model

a place to begin is in determining the contribution made by the program to the development of more and better community leaders. A clear, coherent program logic model provides great assistance during evaluation design. A model points out the key features and shows the relationships that need assessment.

In this example, an evaluation could consider both changes in the awareness, knowledge, skills, and behavior of participants as well as the community development impact. Stakeholders (funders, participants, and other influentials) might also want to know about the content selection and quality of training. They might be curious about implementation fidelity and adaptation, too. Figure 1.3 demonstrates a program logic model with typical evaluation questions.

This program logic model is serving evaluation. The five key evaluation questions are applied at specific locations on the illustrated program model. Key questions for the Community Leadership Academy (CLA) displayed include:

1. Is the CLA doing the right things?

2. Is the CLA doing things right?

3. What difference has the CLA made among participants?

4. What difference has the CLA made across the community?

5. What are the ways community needs can and should be addressed by the CLA?

Positioning questions on the program model identifies where evaluative evidence might be found to address inquiry. Labeling on the model also helps to establish the relationship between program, implementation (processes), results, and evaluation. Question 1 "tests" the logic constructed during evidence based planning. This question requires thoughtful connections be drawn across activity accomplishment, implementation fidelity, and the attainment of desired outcomes/impact. It addresses the overall effectiveness of the selected strategies and related action in achieving the desired results. Question 2 examines implementation fidelity/variance as well as the scope, sequence, penetration, and quality of activities. Questions 3 and 4 focus on the extent to which outcomes and have been achieved. Question 5, like Question 1, should span across the whole model to surface program improvement needs. Questions 1 and 5 are more reflective but essential to improved effectiveness.

These evaluation questions can be very helpful in the initial design and development of the program as they help to aim the program intervention. The next step is establishing indicators. Models also help in guiding the conversation and exploration needed to determine indicators or the measures of progress for an effort. These issues are addressed in greater detail in Chapter 5.

Logic: No Guarantees

It is important to note that the proper reference, "logic model," is *no guarantee* of logic. While many models do demonstrate some modicum of logic, a logical

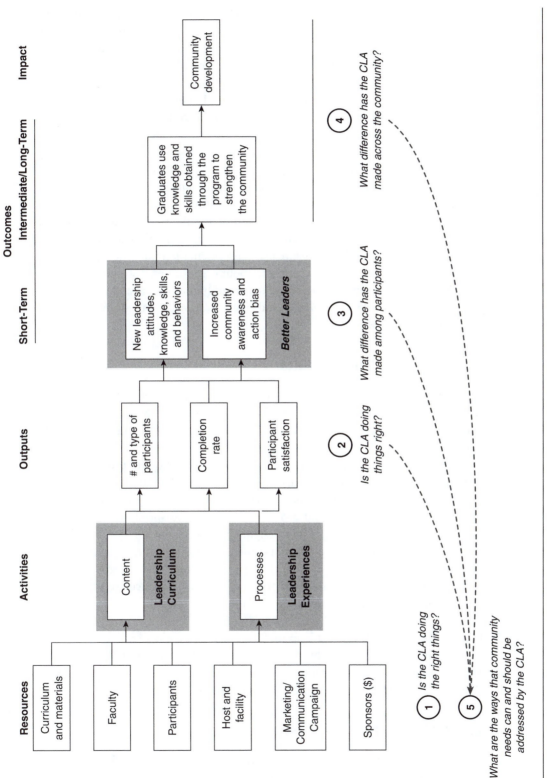

Figure 1.3 Community Leadership Academy (CLA) Program Evaluation Model

representation does not equal plausibility, feasibility, or success. There is some danger in seeing a graphic display on paper and considering it "true." Every model can be considered a draft. The mere existence of a model does not mean that the model or the plans it represents are ready for implementation or that it will readily deliver the intended results!

Chapters 2 and 4 tackle model improvement and development in greater detail. It is essential to note that a model is a graphic display of the program captured at one point in time. Models, we believe, should change to reflect best thinking and current evidence as these evolve. Creating and displaying variations of a model are experiences that can develop thinking about strategies/activities and results. This development is a critical process in model quality and ultimately in the feasibility of the efforts described. We believe the greatest value of logic models is their use in an iterative, intentional process aimed at improving the thinking they illustrate. This is best done through a facilitated sequence with selected stakeholders. Obviously, logic models do not ensure plan implementation fidelity or quality. Nor do they remedy any of the many concerns about organizational structure and culture that can deeply affect program and organizational effectiveness. Important action steps associated with quality include identification of both assumptions and evidence used in models.

Models Begin With Results

Determining the results you desire is the first step in effectiveness because knowing where you are headed is critical to picking the best route to use. In our experience, models begin with results. Results consist of outcomes and impact; each appears in a sequence over time. While impact is the ultimate end sought, sometimes synonymous with vision, outcomes are earlier indications of progress toward results. We think results are the place to begin when you are struggling with choices about strategies (with a theory of change) or activities (with a program logic model). It is important to avoid moving prematurely to specify what you want to do. In any change work, program design, or problem solving, specifying those outcomes most likely to occur soon and then those that will take more time to emerge helps determine what route (action path) might be best to use.

People commonly complain their work is both activity-focused and frantic. Considerable time and effort are spent on a flurry of tasks that frequently lack a clear relationship to intended results. Logic models can assist in sorting priorities because they both rely on and help build a visual literacy that makes action and expected consequence clear. Through the models and modeling, stakeholders can identify potent strategies/activities likely to contribute to the results sought. And those with less (relative) value can be sidelined or discarded.

Logic Models and Effectiveness

In the workplace (and in life), almost everyone is interested in effectiveness. To that end, we provoke important thinking when we ask these questions:

- Are you doing the right work?
- Can you make better decisions?
- Are you getting superior results?

All of these questions apply in any context—whether it is in government or in the private or the nonprofit sector. They are among the most critical questions for managers and leaders because they focus on key levers that influence performance. We know from practical experience and assessment that doing the *right work* along with *great decisions* secures *superior results.* Logic models can help with the design that ensures the right work, the plans and implementation that reflect better decisions, and the evaluation that tests both pathways and progress toward success. For these reasons, they are an exciting tool and process for anyone interested in more effective programs, projects, and organizations.

Figure 1.4 demonstrates key points of the design, planning, implementation, and evaluation that the two types of models can support. Theory of change models are most helpful during the design of a program or project. As plans or evaluation require greater detail, program logic models can make a substantial contribution to these later stages of work. The types of models and their uses form a continuous loop that can provide feedback about a program throughout its life cycle.

Logic models as both a tool and a strategic process offer considerable value to programs and, subsequently, organization effectiveness. They can be used for different purposes at different times in the life cycle of an idea (program, project, or change effort). Theory of change models can dramatically influence program planning because they rely on knowledge to offer choices about doing the right work. In

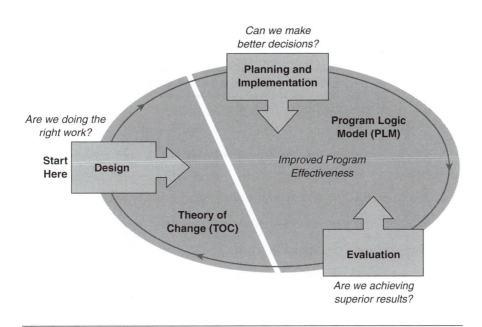

Figure 1.4   Effectiveness and Logic Models

this stage, the selection of strategies relative to results occurs. Program logic models help with more precise decisions about which activities in a given strategy are most effective. Program logic models can also be used to support evaluation design. They can assist in pointing to optimal areas of inquiry and help to determine whether progress is being made and what difference has occurred relative to results.

Some organizations use logic models routinely. They can become a standard tool that promotes alignment and synergy. For example, evaluation can be designed and implemented more easily when a clear theory of change and program logic model have already been determined. These tools and related processes can also assist learning and dissemination in significant ways. Logic models and modeling can be a vital element in performance management because they rely on evidence, support informed decisions about strategy, and assist with assessment. Performance management seeks predetermined results and adapts actions to obtain them.

In Summary

Logic models are simply a visual display of the pathways from actions to results. They are a great way to review and improve thinking, find common understandings, document plans, and communicate and explicate what works under what conditions. We think theory of change models are distinct from program logic models in several important ways. Theory of change models present a very high-level and simple explanation of "do and get." Program logic models offer a detailed map that can be implemented when supplemented with work plans. In this chapter, we also distinguished between models as tools and modeling as a process. A quality feature of logic models is that they are evidence based. Logic models can be used for learning, improving, and greater effectiveness.

Learning Resources

Reflection

1. In what circumstances can you use logic models in your work or field of study?

2. What benefits does each type of model provide? And to whom?

3. What do logic models display? And what is missing?

4. How are theory of change models and program models alike? Different?

5. What kind of logic models have you seen before? Which are most commonly used?

6. What current models/processes are commonly used for program design in your organization? What work cultures are best suited for logic models?

Application

Select and draw one of the following: promotion of a new brand of ketchup, a driver's training program, or a domestic violence awareness campaign. Have others independently draw the same project you select. What do all the drawings have in common? What areas are different? Why? When and how do these differences become reconciled? How did the levels of detail differ among the drawings? What can these drawings tell us about mental maps?

References and Supplemental Readings

Texts

Chen, H. (2005). *Practical program evaluation: Assessing and improving planning, implementation and effectiveness.* Thousand Oaks, CA: Sage.

Fullan, M. (2001). *The new meaning of educational change* (3rd ed.). New York: Teachers College Press.

Kane, M., & Trochim, W. M. K. (2006). *Concept mapping for planning and evaluation.* Thousand Oaks, CA: Sage.

Practical Concepts, Inc. (1971). *The logical framework. Approach and training materials developed for the U.S. Agency for International Development.* Washington, DC. Unpublished manuscript.

United Way of America. (1996). *Measuring program outcomes: A practical approach.* Alexandria, VA: Author.

W. K. Kellogg Foundation. (2001). *The logic model development guide.* Battle Creek, MI: Author. Retrieved October 25, 2007, from http://www.wkkf.org/Pubs/tools/Evaluation/Pub3669.pdf

Weiss, C. H. (1995). *Evaluation* (2nd ed.). Upper Saddle River, NJ: Prentice Hall.

Journal Articles

Bennett, C. (1976). *Analyzing impacts of extension programs, ESC-575.* Washington, DC: U.S. Department of Agriculture, Extension Service.

Fitzpatrick, J. (2002). A conversation with Leonard Bickman. *American Journal of Evaluation, 23*(3), 69–80.

Funnell, S. (1997). Program logic: An adaptable tool for designing and evaluating programs. *Evaluation News and Comment, 6*(1), 5–17.

Internet Resources

Davies, R. (2007). Working with the logical framework (under duress or by desire). *Monitoring and Evaluation News.* Retrieved October 25, 2007, from http://www.mande.co.uk/logframe.htm

Evaluation logic model bibliography. (n.d.). Madison, WI: University of Wisconsin Extension Service. Retrieved October 25, 2007, from http://www.uwex.edu/ces/pdande/evaluation/evallogicbiblio.html

Israel, G. D. (2001). *Using logic models for program development.* Retrieved October 25, 2007, from http://edis.ifas.ufl.edu/WC041

List, D. (2006). *Program logic: An introduction.* Retrieved October 25, 2007, from http://www
.audiencedialogue.net/proglog.html

McCawley, P. F. (1997). *The logic model for planning and evaluation.* Retrieved October 25,
2007, from http://www.uidaho.edu/extension/LogicModel.pdf

CHAPTER 2

Building and Improving Theory of Change Logic Models

This chapter identifies the basic elements of a theory of change logic model. They are evidence based and plausible. This chapter describes the steps to create and improve a theory of change model. It also names criteria for a "good" model.

Learner Objectives

- Identify basic elements of a theory of change model
- Identify the contributions a theory of change model lends to a change effort
- Create a simple theory of change model
- Apply critical review for theory of change model plausibility

Logic models offer an exciting way to combine narrative and graphics to display the mental maps people hold about a specific program or change initiative. These mental constructs are also sometimes called "idea maps." While the process of creating a model can be solitary, there are significant benefits when models are generated in a small group among stakeholders with a shared agenda. Logic models can be used over the entire life of a change effort—their boundaries should be consciously determined by the participants who create the model.

Building a Theory of Change Model

Getting Started

While logic models can be used for many purposes, there are two basic types: theory of change and program models. Understanding these types is important to their development and use. The choice of which to use reflects whether the model needs to describe broad and general concepts about change or more detailed operational elements essential to design, plans, and management. It is possible to begin with either a program logic model or theory of change model.

We believe it is important that a program model always accompany a theory of change because the assumptions held in the theory of change have fundamental value for program operations and success. These assumptions should be consistent and anchor choices made in the development and selection of strategies to fulfill intended results. When assumptions are evidence based, then a single coherent logic and alignment can occur that enables success. Relying on knowledge, whether theory, research, practice, and/or literature, is essential to a good model.

Preferences and Styles

People vary considerably in what level of detail they prefer to describe their mental maps. This is an important consideration for those who lead the modeling process. Invariably, any small group will include people with a strong preference to start at a broad, high level and those who feel far more comfortable beginning with detail. Both approaches have value because the best program or change effort design eventually should display models with these features. Accommodating differences in how any individual approaches the display task is a common tension in the creation process.

Our aim is to guide you consciously from big ideas to finer points. For this reason, we provide a theory of change model description and example first, then a parallel representation of a program logic model in the next chapter. So that content matter does not confound process, we have chosen to use community leadership development and health improvement for all model content in Chapters 1 through 5. A broad range of subject content is offered in the models found in Chapters 6 and 7.

Evidence Based and Plausible

Theories of change can be grounded in either an established claim with proof or in a hypothesis. Programs based on proofs are a replication of something that has worked. Hypotheses are a rationale based on research literature that shows promise of working and is therefore something worth trying. Programs based on hypotheses are innovations. If the theory of change is supported by a body of evidence, there is a stronger chance that the strategies chosen will secure the desired results. Frequently, however, this "standard" is overlooked. In the urgent fever to get to implementation, the design and plan quality can be shortchanged and rely, instead, on faulty assumptions, old practice, little or no evidence.

We suggest practitioners construct the theory of change model with grounding in literature, experience, or other evidence that promotes plausibility. Most theories of change will exhibit some degree of logic. Plausibility, however, is a more appropriate litmus test for work that has inherent opportunity cost. Later, in Chapter 3, we suggest that the program model must also be feasible if there are authentic intentions of securing results. During the construction of a change model, it is important to explore or discover what works under what conditions. This is about the choices made in selection of strategies relative to anticipated and therefore planned results. When constructing a program logic model, the realistic criterion of limited resources is also in play. Any program, project, initiative, or organization has some limits on time, talent, and financial resources. In the migration from theory of change to program logic model, users can shift their thinking from what "could work" to what "should work."

The Big Picture

A theory of change logic model offers the big picture of strategies that could generate your intended results (or impact). This construct is illustrated by Figure 2.1.

A basic theory of change model contains just two elements: strategies and results. The intent is to illustrate the connection between what you will do with what you hope to get.

Strategies reflect a choice of optimal actions (via activities or tactics) to secure intended results. They represent an allocation of resources focused on a clearly defined objective. Marketing, training, political advocacy, and fund development are examples of common strategies. This element describes your actions, or what you plan/propose to "do."

In the private sector, the meaning of strategy is crystal clear. Strategy is the overall plan that gives coherence and purpose to the specific actions that organizations undertake. For some nonprofits, however, the meaning can be murkier and framed as an ambiguous aspiration. When we use the term *strategy,* we rely on an implicit, but evidence-based, assertion that connects means and ends. Wherever the word strategy appears in our illustrations and narrative, we assume that the "business case" for selection is sound. In other words, that it has strong potential to secure impact. Later, in Chapter 3, we also use the term as an umbrella for nested clusters of activities that aim at specific single outcomes or clusters of outcomes.

Results reflect the long-term effect of strategies. They are the "get" from what we are doing. Results are ultimately secured through the change(s) generated by the preceding strategies. They can reflect a single outcome or multiple outcomes over time.

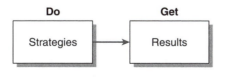

Figure 2.1   Basic Theory of Change

Multiple Strategies and Results

In reality, many programs are more complex than is shown in Figure 2.1. Most often several strategies combined together (over time) in a particular sequence yield results. And we generally both create and experience "results" as the net yield of several strategies working together. When displaying theory of change models this can be challenging both to conceptualize and to represent. For example, to become proficient in a new language, it is most likely the combination of instruction, practice, and cultural immersion that generates proficiency. Likewise, to be a profitable cereal company may require a high level of competency in research/development, marketing, production, and distribution strategies. In addition, great health outcomes for neurosurgery may rely on expertise in diagnostics, surgical techniques, pre- and post-surgical care, and rehabilitation therapies. Because multiple strategies often contribute to results, a more complex representation of a theory of change might look like Figure 2.2. We call the path from each strategy to result a "strand."

Recall the theory of change model for the Community Leadership Academy (Figure 1.1). In that example, the outcome desired was "more and better" community leaders. This model described two simple strategies as essential contributions to the recipe: curriculum and experiences. An applied example of a multi-strategy model for securing "improved health" is displayed in Figure 2.3. Read from left to right, the theory of change suggests *if* we provide exercise, nutrition, stress reduction, and some other key strategies, *then* we will secure improved health for participants who follow the program. It is also important to note that strategies may interact (although not shown here). This theory of change represents a generalized construct for many health improvement programs.

Figure 2.3 simply provides a gross summary of strategies and intended results for a health improvement program. A theory of change model displays some of the

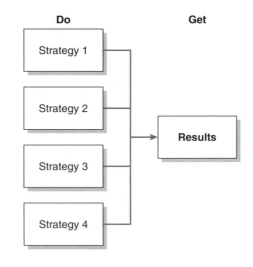

Figure 2.2   Multiple Strategy Basic Theory of Change

Figure 2.3   Health Improvement Theory of Change

underlying assumptions about change and is a view at 65,000 feet. This view is how a farm looks from an airplane window in contrast to the view from a tractor seat. It simply shows the specific strategies that the designer believes will achieve a desired result. Theory of change models are distinct in that they include assumptions (either explicitly or implicitly), offer the "big picture" of the bounded mental map, and name impact. Theory of change models do not provide the detail essential to action planning, implementation, or evaluation. They simply state what you plan to do and what you expect to get. It is easier to explore ideas and manipulate them at this stage. The why and how of these models are embedded in assumptions and eventually reveal themselves in the strategies selected. For example, in Figure 2.3, some of the underlying assumptions might include the following:

- Increased exercise and improved nutrition are known to contribute to improved health.
- Only those who participate in the program will achieve results. Participants need to be recruited.
- Stress may be a contributing factor to poor health.
- Participants' fidelity to the program is critical to achieve results. They will need parallel increases in awareness, knowledge, and skill in order to change behaviors that most impact health.

Realistic Models

Theory of change models should demonstrate plausibility. This means they "could work." Given the realities of limited time, as well as human and social resources, logic alone is inadequate. In fact, the logic displayed in a model can be uninformed or misinformed. For example, world peace is a tangible and clear desired result, but a theory of change that relies solely on communication (e.g., newsletters and Web sites) is not plausible. Or consider the desired result of hiring more mid-level scientists at your research institute. Are "outreach strategies" with local math and science teachers and students logical action steps? Yes, but meetings with those targets can be helpful only in a pipeline that can tolerate a decade of delay. It is not a plausible strategy given urgent human resource needs this week and next month.

Knowledge and Assumptions

So far, we have described a basic theory of change model for improved health that is specifically composed of *doing* (strategies) and *getting* (results). Each of us brings along some other contributions to our theory of change that are more closely held. While not often named, we commonly bring what we *believe* (our assumptions) to theories of change, too. The most viable assumptions used to select strategies are rooted in knowledge, and that knowledge generally includes research, practice, and theory. Figure 2.4 illustrates the knowledge base for beliefs that precedes assumptions and strategies in a theory of change.

It is critical to recognize the role of beliefs. They are important determinants in choices about strategies for both creating and improving a theory of change model. Figure 2.4 illustrates how knowledge and beliefs contribute to a program's underlying or driving assumptions. Assumptions are often informed by knowledge, which can include research, practice, and theory. We find that making assumptions explicit can improve our chances for program success. Sometimes assumptions are informed by experiences, habits, or values that do not also reflect knowledge. Mediating or moderating factors such as program context are useful to consider as barriers or facilitators to program success at this stage. Dogma, misinformation, ignorance, and wishful thinking are hazards here. Often, assumptions can differ significantly among and between both stakeholders who create and those who

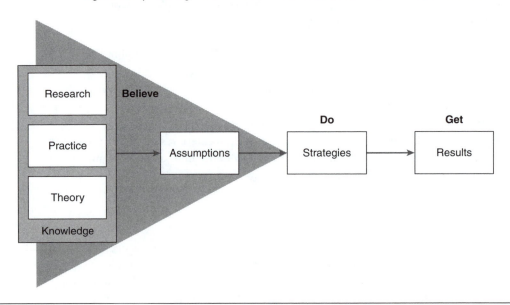

Figure 2.4   Informing a Theory of Change

execute. Modeling can help surface those differences and offer a disciplined process for resolution based first on plausibility, then on feasibility during subsequent versions. This is why, in part, modeling offers considerable value beyond the construction of models alone.

Action Steps: Creating a Theory of Change Logic Model

We recommend that people begin building a theory of change model by specifying their intended results. Most often, it is easiest to be clear first about the intended results. Our experience with clients is they *know* what they want to accomplish. They often label this as desired results.

Once results are named, we suggest identifying the strategies required to achieve the results you seek. Strategies are about *how* intended changes will occur. And assumptions are the preceding knowledge: the research, practice, and theory that inform choices about strategies. They significantly influence which strategies are chosen as pathways to your intended result.

So, the steps to generate a theory of change logic model are ordered in this way:

1. Identify results desired.

2. Name the strategies that will deliver your intended results.

3. Define the assumptions (see Figure 2.4) that support your specified strategies.

Figure 2.5 displays these actions in a 3-step sequence.

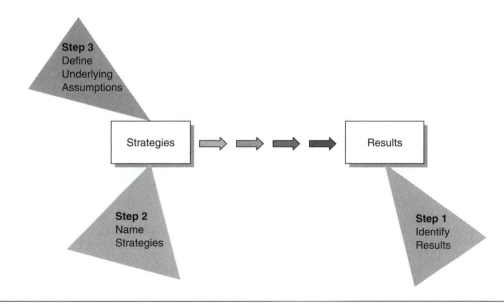

Figure 2.5   Steps in Creating a Theory of Change Model

Most theory of change models generally do not display underlying beliefs or assumptions. Nevertheless, these are important elements to explore consciously when creating a theory of change. We suggest those assumptions are named in association with the theory of change. Assumptions can simply be a bulleted list on the same page or reverse side. Remember, a theory of change model is simply one representation of the "truth," not a substitute for it. The model draft becomes a place for starting discussion and testing meaning, coherence, assumptions, and plausibility. Engaging others in modeling offers the opportunity for critical review and improvement over time through the generation of versions. By starting with a theory of change model, it is easier to arrive at shared understanding of what your program will do and can achieve.

Improving Theory of Change Models

We offer several common processes to consider as you explore iterations of your theory of change model. While improvement is definitely not limited to these suggestions, an application of these four will likely contribute to the development of any attempt:

- Engage multiple stakeholders.
- Share explicit assumptions.
- "Toggle" or test alternative content in model versions.
- Explore promising practices and consider benchmarking.

Multiple Perspectives

People hold and operationalize theories of change in both their work and personal lives. Most experienced parents, for example, have a recipe that contains the primary strategies they believe are vital to parenting a "good kid." Parents can vary considerably, however, in what they mean by a good kid. Likewise, even if we agree on what a good kid might know and be able to do, it is highly likely that from one parent to the next, there will be many variations on parenting strategies to ensure the "good kid" result. This example suggests the considerable importance of ensuring that all stakeholders in your program or change effort are specifying results and the strategies needed to get there with the same meaning and level of specificity. Developing and improving the theory of change for your program is one way to begin the conversations needed to reach shared understanding.

In the health example we started this chapter with (see Figure 2.3), we identify "improved health" as the result sought. It is important to ensure that everyone has a highly consistent understanding of what "improved health" means. To one participant, it may be weight loss. Another could interpret it as normal blood pressure. Others may feel improved health is a combination of several positive outcomes. If you ask a half-dozen people what improved health means to them, it is quite likely there will be variation in their individual answers.

Specifying what the results mean, such as improved health in this example, becomes critical for both your program design as well as essential for measuring progress toward and determination of results. If the meaning and measures of results are shared and understood similarly, then it is more likely strategy choices will align with your intended impact. It is more likely indicators of progress will be appropriate, too.

"Unpack" and Share Assumptions

The most significant opportunity to improve theory of change models lies in unpacking the knowledge and beliefs employed in assumptions. This means, in practice, that any theory of change for a program or social change effort should be grounded in knowledge. If results are connected to strategies that reflect research, practice, theory, and experience—there are far greater chances for success than with strategies that lack this grounding. Figure 2.6 displays a combination of the elements found in knowledge. A combination of little or no practice, experience, research, and theory in your model means the effort it represents is an idea that may be highly innovative but is not likely to succeed. A combination of practice, experience, research, and theory in your model suggests the effort it represents is more likely to succeed.

The best theory of change model *deliberately pursues* alignment among research, theory, practice, and experience. The stronger models build on the knowledge and good work that precedes them. These substantiated models and their associated programs or social change efforts gather and then use codified knowledge from prior efforts to inform effective program design. Figure 2.6 describes the geography of choices and emphasizes that relative success relies on a depth of practice, experience, research, and theory.

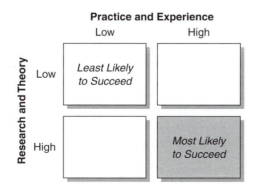

Figure 2.6   Success in Theory of Change Models

Toggling

Another practical way to improve models is what we refer to as "toggling." We define toggling as finding the optimal fit between a selected set of strategies and plausible results. For example, options to improve school nutrition could include planting a garden, removing vending machines, or changing the lunch menu. Toggling "tries on" options and makes a best choice. In this critical review, the model builder is experimenting with the best combination of strategies to secure the results sought. Inviting others to join in this iterative tactic in real time can be very productive. Sometimes it is best to refine or focus the specified results. For example, a program or social change effort could specify one of these results: "end childhood obesity" or "create schools with improved nutrition choices for children." During toggling, it may become apparent the result is not plausible. Often, ambitions are greater than what is feasible. It is important to guard against grand ambitions. They are possible hazards that can result in flawed models. Figure 2.7 demonstrates the interactions between strategies and results as choices are made in the final determination.

This figure displays the "testing" that occurs in an effort to determine the best combination of strategies to secure your intended results. Once a preliminary theory of change model is drawn, the modeling process begins. The model is tested though iterative cycles of inquiry. The basic questions addressed are, "Are the results focused and narrow enough to discern optimum strategies?" and "Is the connection between the strategies named and the results desired as strong and direct as needed to be effective with the population of interest?"

Toggling can also involve a review of both the duration and sequence for chosen strategies. The objective is to specify a model that is plausible. The specifics of what is feasible are developed in the program logic model (and is discussed in following chapters). People sometimes mention confusion when they talk about the "fog of war." In our experience, there is considerable "fog" or ambiguity in program design and planning. A clear and plausible theory of change is the foundation of intended work and requires considerable attention and scrutiny. Just as with the Cheshire Cat in the story *Alice in Wonderland,* if you do not know where you are going, any road will do. Fuzzy, ambiguous theories of change rarely net the success intended.

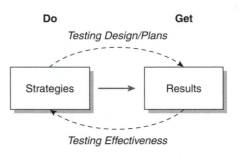

Figure 2.7   "Toggle": Improving Theory of Change Models

Promising Practices and Benchmarking

It is valuable to explore strategies and results of programs (or social change efforts) similar to yours. A better understanding of the rationale for their strategies and related results can deeply inform your design choices. In the private sector, this is often referred to as "benchmarking," a systematic discovery and comparison process that can be a simple way of *both* clarifying and improving your design early on. In benchmarking, one simply looks around at promising practices to inform and then make good choices about your own. Benchmarking may include a review of documents, a survey, and discovery with peers/competitors. It establishes the status of other efforts, programs, or organizations on specified features or issues. The big questions benchmarking can help answer are what others are doing and why? Chapter 7 provides some examples of archetypes, general recipes that are evidence based, that can also help in your early efforts to construct a model.

School improvement efforts, for example, often include quality instructional and assessment practices among their many strategies aimed at teachers to, ultimately, improve student academic achievement. There is evidence these strategies can positively influence academic student achievement. It follows that a school improvement effort, then, might be more successful if these strategies (or some adapted version) are included in the program plan. The converse is also true. A school without these strategies as standard operating procedure or as part of a new plan is less likely to secure improved academic student achievement. A theory of change can show what you are and are not thinking about. The accompanying modeling process provides the opportunity to reflect and improve on the underlying "logic" for your program.

As you construct, then review a theory change, the following questions may be useful:

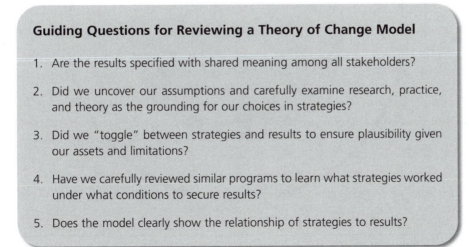

Guiding Questions for Reviewing a Theory of Change Model

1. Are the results specified with shared meaning among all stakeholders?

2. Did we uncover our assumptions and carefully examine research, practice, and theory as the grounding for our choices in strategies?

3. Did we "toggle" between strategies and results to ensure plausibility given our assets and limitations?

4. Have we carefully reviewed similar programs to learn what strategies worked under what conditions to secure results?

5. Does the model clearly show the relationship of strategies to results?

Nonlinear Theory of Change Models

Theory of change logic models are not always displayed in a linear fashion (as they have been in the text so far). Realistically, few theories, programs, or change efforts occur in a precisely linear sequence. The world is much more complicated and integrated than the simple, step-by-step actions and reactions as drawn here. Most change occurs iteratively, or in cycles, and with multiple interaction among many features. Any change is also connected to a much larger system than illustrated by the theory of change model. In our experience, systems and holism can be difficult to manage and even harder to evaluate or communicate. In generating a theory of change, it is important represent how change occurs as an aspect of a far more comprehensive and vast geography. When using a systems view, it is important to consider the key leverage points or strategies that are most influential given time, expertise, and resources. A simple example of a nonlinear theory of change logic model is shown in Figure 2.8.

In Figure 2.8, the four strategies that contribute to results occur in a specific sequence over and over again. Their interaction contributes to the center target: results, an aggregate of progress over time. The intersection and influence of external issues and/or the environment can be illustrated as well.

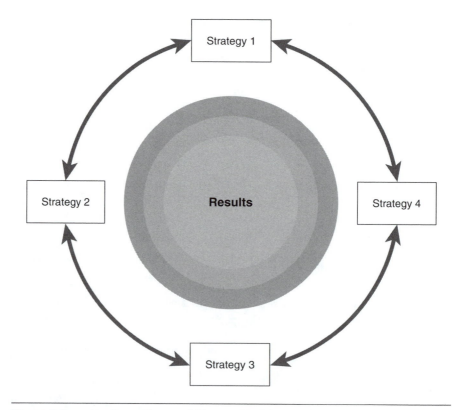

Figure 2.8   Nonlinear Theory of Change Model

In the nonlinear theory of change model, Figure 2.9 represents an alternative view of the Community Leadership Academy theory of change model shown earlier. Through two strategies identified here—curriculum and experiences—this change efforts expects to produce "more and better" community leaders and, ultimately, community development. The curriculum, the experiences, and the participants interact. Chapters 6 and 7 also provide some additional examples of nonlinear models.

Doing the "Right Work"

In Chapter 1, we mentioned effectiveness and three critical questions:

- Are you doing the right work?
- Can you make better decisions?
- Are you getting superior results?

The first question was about the "right work." This is about attending to making the strongest, most direct, and plausible connection between your strategies and results. It is about the focus of time, energy, talents, and resources in relation to your

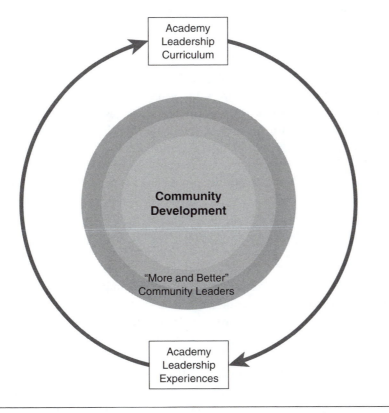

Figure 2.9   Community Leadership Academy Nonlinear Theory of Change Model

specified success. Eventually, right work is also about detailing those specific activities that are subsumed by each strategy that is chosen for display in the program logic model. Giving conscious attention to the criterion used in selecting strategies at this stage and again later when using the program logic model to identify how implementation can make a big difference in the likelihood of your program or change effort to secure results. The right work is clarified and confirmed if there is a shared understanding of the problem you plan to resolve and there is agreement on how it can be accomplished. Specificity here, on the front end, contributes to the results you and your colleagues intend to secure. Ambiguity can doom the best-intentioned efforts to failure.

If your end result in a construction project is a great house, then cooking and sewing probably are not the most relevant strategies. However, planning with well-detailed blueprints as well as appropriate purchasing (e.g., quality lumber) and contracting should be ripe for your attention. It is surprisingly easy to spend time on the wrong work. It can be an unconscious or conscious choice. Theory of change models should display planned results and specify the most relevant and influential strategies to secure the results. The strategies are determined from a universe of possibilities. Often, people include strategies (and later, activities) they have always done or are most familiar with doing. If replication is intentional, then repeating what has been done before might be appropriate. As time passes and knowledge changes, however, results may require we use what has been learned about new or different strategies (and activities) to be more efficient and effective. Remember, a theory is only as good as its last test.

Tough Questions

Of course, there are many ways to secure a named and intended result. Discarding strategies/activities that are peripheral, modest contributors or less than optimal in potency can focus limited resources. Models and their iterations can develop a disciplined way of thinking that contributes to new understandings about what will generate progress toward results. Once results are specified, the discovery and discussion that should be encouraged during your modeling attends to these two big questions:

- What are the many ways we could resolve this challenge?
- Then, what are the most effective and efficient ways to secure results?

Subsequently, as model versions are explored, it is important to inquire further. For example: Are we doing something that has a reasonable chance of working? Are we doing something that should be done? Are we clear enough about the work that we have shared expectations for what it includes and can yield? How does our model rely on research, practice, theory, and/or literature? We know that the politics of power and dynamics of resources often preclude these conversations. A predisposition to activities and busyness can overwhelm a disciplined and interactive process, too. However, the benefits and relative value of getting things "right" at the start are considerable. The opportunity cost or waste in missing this step is huge.

In Summary

Logic models display mental maps people hold about cause and effect. Combined, theory of change coupled with program logic models are the most potent design prescription. Theory of change models specify and link strategies with results. Most change efforts require multiple strategies. Knowledge is a critical input for models and can include research, practice, and theory. What people believe affects the content and format of models. Improving theory of change models requires multiple perspectives, unpacking assumptions, shared language, toggling, and the exploration of promising practices.

Learning Resources

Reflection

1. What role do assumptions and beliefs play in a theory of change model?

2. How can you "test" a theory of change model for plausibility? Why bother with this step?

3. Are there blind spots in the modeling process? If so, what are they?

4. What are the implications of a change model that relies on a hypothesis versus one based on a claim with proof?

5. What are some ways that theory of change models can be improved and/or developed?

6. What challenges do complex and highly interactive systems present in a theory of change model? Where and how do you bound the presentation of a theory of change model?

Application

1. Have a conversation:
   A. Ask colleagues to share their beliefs about parenting (or their mothers' or fathers' beliefs) to ensure a happy, confident, successful young adult. From this conversation, draw a theory of change. What are their most important strategies? Can you identify their beliefs, values, assumptions? Do they cite any evidence for their choices? Is research, practice, or theory part of their explanation? How are their views similar to or different from yours? Do they have a shared understanding and agreement about parenting with their spouse (or among their parents)? How does your response to these questions influence the model?
   B. Ask a friend or colleague to share a recipe for marketing a new car model. What are the most important strategies for ensuring profit? What evidence

supports their choice of strategies? How do assumptions inform their theory of profitability? How does your response to these questions influence the model?

2. Ask several people to list the many ways that "improved health" might be described. Why does this outcome/result have different meanings? Could these differences influence modeling?

3. Find a news article that describes a change effort (in government, nonprofit, or private sector). Draw it. Can you detect the efforts underlying theory of change? How was it informed: based on a claim or a hypothesis?

4. Considering the drawings from 1 and 3 above, how do choices of strategies influence the likelihood of achieving your intended results? What changes, if any, could be made to improve the plausibility of these models?

References and Supplemental Readings

Texts

Chen, H. T. (1994). *Theory-driven evaluations.* Thousand Oaks, CA: Sage.

Donaldson, S. I. (2007). *Program theory-driven evaluation science: Strategies and applications.* Mahwah, NJ: Lawrence Erlbaum.

Porter, M. E. (1995). *Competitive advantage: Creating and sustaining superior performance.* New York: Free Press.

Weiss, C. H. (1995). *Evaluation* (2nd ed.). Upper Saddle River, NJ: Prentice Hall.

Weiss, C. H. (1995). Nothing as practical as a good theory. In J. P. Connell, A. C. Kubisch, L. B. Schorr, & C. H. Weiss. (Eds.). *New approaches to evaluating community initiatives: Concepts, methods and contexts* (pp. 65–92). Washington, DC: Aspen Institute.

Reisman, J., & Gienapp, A. (2004). *Theory of change: A practical tool for action, results and learning.* Baltimore, MD: Annie E. Casey Foundation. Retrieved October 25, 2007, from http://www.aecf.org/upload/PublicationFiles/CC2977K440.pdf

Journal Articles

Birckmayer, J. D., & Weiss, C. H. (2000). Theory-based evaluation in practice: What do we learn? *Evaluation Review, 24*(8), 40–43.

Bolduc, K., Buteau, E., Laughlin, G., Ragin, R., & Ross, J. A. (n.d.). *Beyond the rhetoric: Foundation strategy.* Cambridge, MA: Center for Effective Philanthropy. Retrieved April 24, 2008, from http://www.effectivephilanthropy.org/images/pdfs/CEP_Beyond_the_Rhetoric.pdf

Donaldson, S. I. (2001). Mediator and moderator analysis in program development. In S. Sussman (Ed.), *Handbook of program development for health behavior research and practice* (pp. 470–496). Thousand Oaks, CA: Sage.

Kramer, M. R. (2001, May/June). Strategic confusion. *Foundation News and Commentary, 42*(3). Retrieved April 24, 2008, from http://www.foundationnews.org/CME/article.cfm?ID=847

Monroe, M. C., Fleming, M. L., Bowman, R. A., Zimmer, J. F., Marcincowski, T., Washburn, J., & Mitchell, N. J. (2005). Evaluators as educators: Articulating program theory and building evaluation capacity. *New Directions for Evaluation, 108,* 57–71.

Rogers, P. J., Petrosino, A., Huebner, T. A., & Hacsi, T. A. (2000). Program theory evaluation: Practice, promise, and problems. *New Directions for Evaluation, 87,* 5–13.

Sridharan, S., Campbell, B., & Zinzow, H. (2006). Developing a stakeholder-driven anticipated timeline of impact for evaluation of social programs. *American Journal of Evaluation, 27*(6), 148–162.

Internet Resources

For a comprehensive Web site and online suite of tools sponsored by ActKnowledge and the Aspen Institute on Community Change, see:

Theory of change. (n.d.). Retrieved October 25, 2007, from http://www.theoryofchange.org

CHAPTER 3

Creating Program Logic Models

This chapter identifies the basic elements of a program logic model. Generally, these models have enough detail to support design, planning, management, or evaluation. This chapter describes a program logic model example and the action steps to create a model with a small group.

Learner Objectives

- Describe the relationship between theory of change and program logic models
- Identify basic elements for a program logic model
- Create a simple model
- Recognize limitations of display

From Theory of Change to Program Models

Theory of change logic models are literally the foundation for program logic models. When well developed, they can ensure intellectual rigor for program logic models. Figure 3.1 illustrates the relationship of a theory of change model (composed of strategies and results) to the primary elements of a program logic model.

Strategies reflect the resources, activities, and outputs needed to achieve results. Results reflect the sequence of outcomes over time through impact. Outcomes (for individuals) are generally progress in changes in awareness, knowledge, skill, or behavior among targeted audiences. There are also outcomes for organizations and systems. Although a plausible and evidence-based connection can be established,

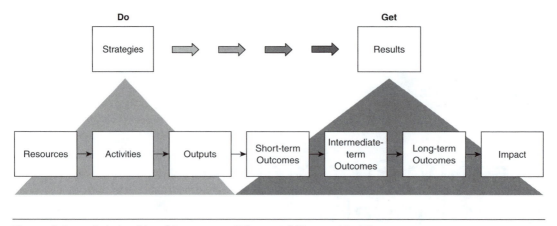

Figure 3.1   Relationship of Program and Theory of Change Models

impact is often well beyond the scope (or feasibility) for the program being modeled. Together, outcomes, which are closer to the effort, of multiple strategies plus impact (further away) make up results. While program logic models are often built on a theory of change, it is also possible to infer a theory of change from a program logic model.

Assumptions Matter

It is important to be aware that specific assumptions are not illustrated in Figure 3.1. Recall that assumptions are informed by beliefs and knowledge. Too often, program models are built without the benefit of explicitly naming the assumptions and underlying theory of change. This omission can help explain why tremendous conflict, even chaos can erupt during program development, planning, implementation, or assessment. In the absence of explicitly named assumptions, either a clear theory of change does not exist or people hold multiple and conflicting variations that reflect their deeply held views about what should/could work and why. This can lead to diffuse or dilute programs that lack the focus and intensity needed to produce intended results. Because of these implications, omitting this "foundation" for your idea, program, or social change effort undermines its potential for success.

As noted previously, conceptualization and learning styles differ from person to person. Organizational culture can also affect how design, planning, monitoring, and measuring occur. Given these practical issues, we strongly suggest that both theory of change and program logic models are eventually created to form the foundation of shared meaning for all aspects of the program. The sequence in which they are developed certainly should and will reflect the stakeholders' preferences.

Key Elements of Program Logic Models

Program logic models display what an existing idea, new program, or focused change effort might contain from start to finish. The elements in a program logic model consist of the recipe for a bounded investment of financial and social capi-tal for a specified result. The level of detail increases so that the relationships shown by the model illustrate essential linkages needed to make a plan fully operational for each of the strategy strands identified in the theory of change. The primary elements for each strand of a program logic model include resources, activities, outputs, outcomes, and impact. Figure 3.2 is a template of the elements for most program logic models.

These program logic model elements are defined as follows:

Resources are essential for activities to occur. They can include human, financial, organizational, community, or systems resources in any combination. They are used to accomplish named activities. Sometimes resources are called inputs.

Activities are the specific actions that make up the program. They reflect tools, processes, events, technology, and other devices that are intentional in the program. Activities are synonymous with interventions deployed to secure the desired changes or results.

Outputs are what specific activities will produce or create. They can include descriptions of types, levels, and audiences or targets delivered by the program. Outputs are often quantified and qualified in some way. They simply characterize the application of activities with selected audiences.

Outcomes are about changes, often in program participants or organizations, as a result of the program. They often include specific changes in awareness, knowl-edge, skill, and behavior. Outcomes are dependent on preceding resources, activi-ties, and outputs. Sometimes outcomes are parsed by time increments into short, intermediate, and long term. Time spans for outcomes are relative and should be specified for the idea or project described. However, short term is often 1 through 3 years, intermediate-term outcomes 4 through 6 years. Long-term outcomes might be achieved in 7 through 10 years. The intervals specified for any given model would depend on the size and scope of the effort.

For example, a small-scale project such as an adult education typing class in one location might produce knowledge and skill outcomes in 6 weeks, where behavior changes such as use or changes in employment might take somewhat longer. Alternatively, a program targeting changes in global water quality might specify changes in the awareness and knowledge of international policymakers within 1 to 3 years; actual environmental improvements might not occur within decades. Typically, dividing the project duration into thirds works pretty well as a starting point. Relying on a literature or other evidence base can help inform what is feasible.

Being clear about timing and expected results is important. The time span for outcomes is project specific. Time is one of several important considerations. The

Figure 3.2   A Basic Program Logic Model

logical sequencing of any given outcome chain matters too. Think about what will happen first, then what is likely to happen next. Also keep in mind that the sequence may or may not be lockstep. Under some conditions, there may be different points of entry into a sequence. The important thing is to explore the interconnections and dependencies that do exist among the outcomes and impact you specify.

Impact is the ultimate intended change in an organization, community, or other system. It carries an implication about time. It varies in its relative timing to the actual program or change effort. Sometimes impact occurs at the end of the program, but more frequently, the impact sought is much more distant. For some efforts, this may mean impact can be cited in 7 through 10 years or more. This can have important implications as it is well beyond the funding cycle for many typical grant-funded programs or the patience of many managers or politicians. The logic model is one way to show how the work you can do within these constraints may contribute to a larger, grander impact.

The "planned work" of a program logic model includes resources, activities, and outputs. These are the essential elements that are used to secure results or make change happen. The "intended results" include what the program produces: outcomes and impact.

Nonlinear Program Logic Models

Just as in theory of change models, very few ideas, programs, or projects actually occur in a linear progression. Purposely, to aid learning, we simplified the display of elements as a straight sequence. Reality suggests cycles, iterations (additional attempts), and interactions are very common. This more organic development is shown in Figure 3.3.

In this circular display, there is no specific starting point. Although the logic model elements are constant, the work of design, planning, managing, or evaluating might begin with any element. In addition, this view shows how cycles of the same activity might occur over time. Keep in mind, the illustration groups activities together. A more detailed view could be staggering to portray. Sometimes, capturing reality in a display impedes communication.

Hidden Assumptions and Dose

A program logic model displays the elements that are most critical to establishing and operating a program or social change effort. It specifies the activities and their often interdependent relationship as well as what they are expected to generate. Program logic models do not necessarily include assumptions, but they rely on them. They offer a view of the map that can inform action planning and, later, implementation. Program logic models can also define the "dose" (e.g., number, type, and duration of activities), quantify and describe the effects and benefits of the program for a given dose and the ultimate change expected. Dose is an important concept in effectiveness. A dilute dose can have the same impact as none at all. For example, if your intended result is a large voter turnout in an election, a classified ad

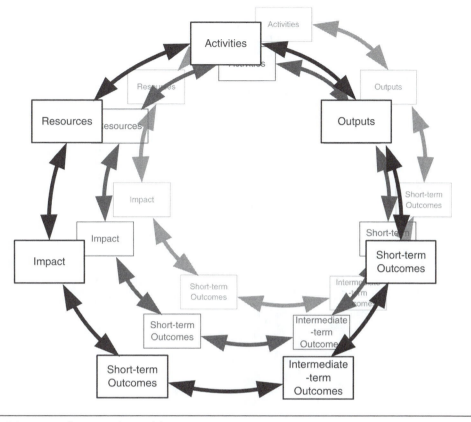

Figure 3.3   Nonlinear Logic Model

is not an adequate communication strategy. A comprehensive media plan coupled with free transportation to the voting booths has greater chances of success. So, it is important to design a program with enough of the right activities to secure the outcome you intend.

Building a Program Logic Model

Program Logic Model Example

An example of a simple program logic model for securing "improved health" is displayed in Figure 3.4. Read from left to right, this program model suggests that if we recruit and retain participants and provide exercise, nutrition, and stress reduction, then we will secure improved health. Note the development of detail connecting strategies to results in this model compared to the theory of change (see Figure 2.3). The program logic model provides detail for the theory of change by explicating the elements from a basic logic model for each strategy strand. In a program model, the details relative to resources, activities, and other elements are named.

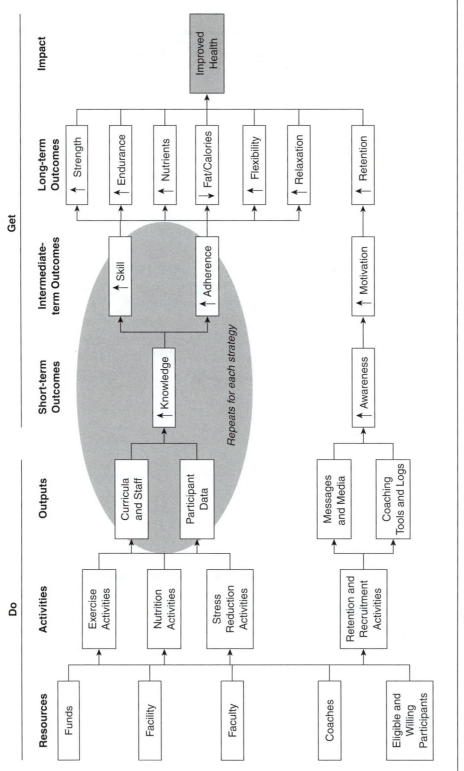

Figure 3.4 Improved Health Program Logic Model

Although still an overview and incomplete, this illustration provides a more detailed view of what this health improvement program wants to do, plans to measure, and hopes to achieve. Beginning on the left with resources, this model includes funds, facility, faculty, coaches, as well as eligible and willing participants among its requisite inputs. To keep it simple, the strategies contain implied clusters of activities in this illustration. The specific activities that contribute to outputs are not named. Outputs from the intervention strategies and associated activities (exercise, nutrition, stress reduction) could be numerous. For this illustration, we show only the overarching categories of information that could be considered. Each category would be repeated for each of the strands. These would include details about the scope, sequence, and quality of the curriculum; staffing qualifications; and information about participants and their participation. Activities "inside" these strategy strands contribute to changes in knowledge, skill, and adherence. Eventually, they can contribute to increases in strength, endurance, nutrients, flexibility, and relaxation. Concurrently, over time, these same strategies also yield reduced fat/calories. The retention and recruitment strategy strand also generates some outputs and outcomes. Aggregated, activities within this strategy secure and keep participants in the program. Note that this model uses arrows to show relationships. Sometimes they reflect a cluster (indicating synergies) rather than just one:one relationships.

As is typical of many programs, several strategies may be shown as contributing collectively to outcomes, rather than each strategy making its individual contribution to distinct outcomes in isolation. Collectively, the long-term outcomes generate improved health, which could be measured in a variety of ways (e.g., blood pressure, blood lipid and sugar profiles, weight).

In contrast to the big picture view that theory of change models offer, program logic models provide a closer, more detailed picture of operations. This view of the program provides adequate detail to then create work plans. Program models can provide a reliable outline for work plans that are used to implement and manage a program or larger change effort. Just like theory of change models, program models are often logical—but here, feasibility, given limited time and resources, is the appropriate standard for assessing their value. A common question about program logic models focuses on their level of detail. Essentially, the level of detail in program logic models should be determined by their intended use and users. Although somewhat situational, program logic models build out strategies to activities. Sometimes they can even get to the fine detail of tasks, although more often that is described in an operations or action plan.

From Strategy to Activities

Some program logic models can be extremely complex, but the steps to create them are generally the same as for more simple efforts (see Figure 3.2). Large-scale programs or multi-year change efforts (sometimes called "initiatives") often are composed of many strategies aimed at target audiences across many sites over considerable time.

Program logic models usually do not display underlying beliefs or assumptions. They are nevertheless important elements in the conscious exploration of multiple target audiences. Sometimes programs or change efforts are implemented in a cascade with some overlap in time, which requires a particular sequence of strategies and associated activities. When this is the circumstance, it can be helpful to focus on a function, a given strategy, or one partner's designated work. The task is often simplified by thinking about a single aspect and then connecting it back to the whole with some of the inherent complexity reduced. Ultimately, program execution relies on integrated action—but the work that precedes it may require focused developmental attention on smaller parts.

Using the health improvement program example, Figure 3.5 provides an orientation to how the exercise strategy strand might be reduced to activities. It breaks the strategy into greater detail for the purposes of selection and design.

In Figure 3.5, it becomes evident that exercise as a strategy is made up of several key activities. They include physical exercise (strength and endurance), education, and assessment. Together, all of these activities represent a comprehensive strategy, exercise, that is just one means to improved health. Recall that the whole theory of change for this example also includes stress reduction, nutrition, and retention. It is the combination of strategies reflected in the whole program that is most likely to secure results. Each strand of a comprehensive program logic model needs to illustrate the contribution of each strategy as well as the interdependence.

As you specify the activities content of your strategy you are naming more precisely what makes up the given strategy. Later, the whole model is tested for feasibility—both practically before implementation and literally when the program is evaluated.

In Figure 3.6, we provide a view with greater detail for *only* the exercise strategy.

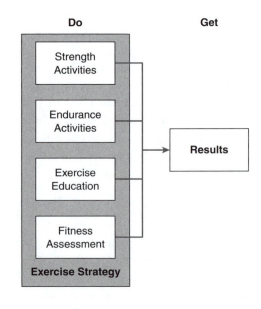

Figure 3.5   One Strategy With Multiple Activities

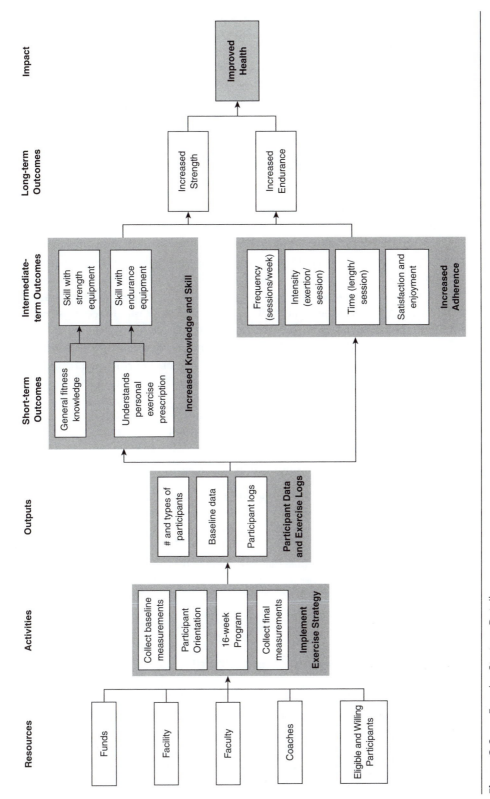

Figure 3.6 Exercise Strategy Detail

In this illustration, we show the detail of activities within the exercise strategy. It also suggests the many decisions hidden in program design and planning. In choosing activities, it is critical that the relationship among strategies and activities is intentional. The strategies and the cluster of appropriate activities should also be chosen with reference to a target audience. Remember, logic models use if–then sequences from left to right in the columns and among the features as you read from left to right.

Action Steps for a Program Logic Model

The practical construction of a program logic model often begins with one or more information sources (e.g., research, interviews, documents). We recommend that people begin both theory of change and program logic models with the named ends. People are most clear about their intended results (outcomes and impact). Our experience is that you do *know* what you want to accomplish. The results sought reflect both the impact intended and the outcomes over time. Next, name the changes or outcomes that will be part of your progress toward impact. Unpacking this sequence is important because it makes it easier to see the strength of the connection between what you do and what you can get. We suggest tackling the activities required to achieve the outcomes you have specified in your third step. Activities are about *how* intended changes will occur. Fourth, resources/inputs become the essential ingredients of activities. And finally, outputs reflect the information needed to verify that activities named earlier in the process reach the right audiences and are of the quality and quantity needed to produce results. So, the steps to draft a program logic model are ordered in this way:

1. Identify the results that one or more strategies will ultimately generate.

2. Describe the stepwise series of outcomes (or changes) that will show progress toward impact.

3. Name all the activities needed to generate the outcomes (for each strategy).

4. Define the resources/inputs that link directly to and will "supply" the activities.

5. Identify the outputs that reflect the accomplishment of activities.

Figure 3.7 illustrates these action steps and their sequence.

Creating Your Program Logic Model

The format of a logic model format helps organize information in a useful way. Think of an idea, project, or program you manage now or want to create and its results. For each strategy, brainstorm elements that might be cited in short-term outcomes first but are clearly linked to your intended results. Do the same for resources, activities, and outputs. It is important to make choices about the outcomes that are feasible with your limited resources. This is discussed in greater detail in the next chapter.

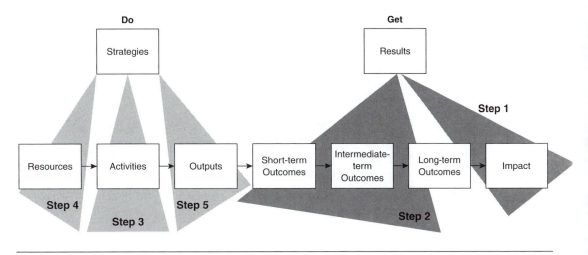

Figure 3.7   Steps in Creating a Program Logic Model

With some experience, you will begin to recognize commonly used strategies that reflect knowledge from your field or discipline. For example, marketing/communication, recruitment, retention, professional development or education, advocacy, and policy are strategies often found in program models. Examples of activities under a marketing/communication strategy could include prepare database of target markets, generate news releases, create and send a newsletter, generate a Web site, and prepare public service announcements. We suggest you tackle one strategy at a time. Aim to define the same level of detail for each strategy. Selected examples of archetypes, or tested recipes, are described in Chapter 7.

Creating a Program Logic Model Together

We think the best method for generating a program logic model engages a small group, especially if the members are stakeholders in the idea or program it represents. Stakeholders are situational, but generally are those with an interest in or people likely to benefit from the program. Logic modeling often includes funders, program staff, and program participants. Intentionally including stakeholders supports best contributions as well as some subsequent benefits relative to implementation. The facilitation of modeling requires some advance planning and a commitment to both discipline and quality during the process. A determination about the status of a shared understanding and meaning for specified results gets your effort started. It is important to note that models may need to be updated to respond to the dynamics of an external environment (context). They also reflect living systems that are not mechanistic but changing. For these two reasons (and others), it is necessary to expect models will be revised. With limits on time, impact and outcomes can be identified and selected. This can be accomplished a number of ways.

We have had success in using the action steps noted, particularly when each participant contributed to the model elements via small sticky notes. This quickly generates a large number of possibilities for each element. Redundancies should be noted and celebrated as commonly held. Then, the group can sort them: those that *must* be kept, that *could* be kept, and those that are *not relevant.* Once the results are named, then it is relatively easy to specify the other elements. In this disciplined process each stakeholder contributes to the whole and each contribution has the benefit of an internal test relative to design.

We often use Microsoft Visio to construct our models, but many other applications such as Word and PowerPoint have drawing options. These as well as Inspiration software are all readily available. The Supplemental Readings list at the end of the chapter identifies some examples of other free and commercial software applications. Take care in using technology for model creation because it can exclude valuable participation.

In Summary

High-quality program logic models depend on the evidence base found in their parallel but simpler theory of change models. Program logic models display several important elements: resources; activities; outputs; short-, intermediate-, and long-term outcomes; and impact. To create a program logic model start with the intended results: outcomes and impact. Then, activities (which are consistent with strategies in the theory of change model) are selected. Next, resources and outputs are cited. We believe creating models with deep participation of stakeholders improves their quality and encourages their use.

Learning Resources

Reflection

1. What are the implications of a program logic model built without a specific theory of change?

2. Think of a successful business and its product or service. What is the underlying program logic that shows the explanations for profitability?

3. Feasibility relies on several aspects. Can you name some?

4. What are strengths and limitations of a linear or a nonlinear display? Would individuals from different fields (and their relevant cultures) answer similarly or differently? Why?

5. Why is being specific about results important?

Application

Specify the result of a shared program, project, or idea. Draw a theory of change model for the program, project, or idea. Then, attempt a program logic model. Using sticky notes or pieces of paper, brainstorm the outcomes that need to happen to secure the result. Organize them into short, intermediate, and long term. Pick one short-term outcome. Brainstorm what activities are critical to that outcome. Organize the activities relative to a single or multiple strategies. For given strategies and their activities, name the resources needed. From the activities, cite what outputs are possible. Organize these elements as one model.

References and Supplemental Readings

Texts

Frechtling, J. (2007). *Logic modeling methods in program evaluation.* San Francisco: Jossey-Bass.

Green, E. L. (2005). *Reinventing logic models: A stakeholder-driven group approach.* Unpublished doctoral dissertation, University of Cincinnati, OH.

Mayeske, G. W. (1994). *Life cycle program management and evaluation: An heuristic approach.* Washington, DC: United States Department of Agriculture.

United Way of America. (1996). *Measuring program outcomes: A practical approach.* Alexandria, VA: Author.

Westley, F., Zimmerman, B., & Patton, M. Q. (2007). *Getting to maybe: How the world is changed.* Toronto: Vintage Canada.

Wong-Rieger, D., & David, L. (1996). *A hands-on guide to planning and evaluation.* Ottawa: Canadian Hemophilia Society.

Journal Articles

Cooksy, L. J., Gill, P., & Kelly, P. A. (2001). The program logic model as an integrative framework for a multimethod evaluation. *Evaluation and Program Planning, 24*(2), 119–128.

McLaughlin, J. A. (1999). Logic models: A tool for telling your program's performance story. *Evaluation and Program Planning, 22*(1), 65–72.

Millar, A., Simeone, R. S., & Carnevale, J. T. (2001). Logic models: A systems tool for performance management. *Evaluation and Program Planning, 24*(1), 73–81.

Rush, B., & Ogborne, A. (1991). Program logic models: Expanding their role and structures for program planning and evaluation. *Canadian Journal of Program Evaluation, 6,* 95–106.

Internet Resources

For comprehensive bibliographies and links to additional resources, see:

Logic model resources. (n.d.). Atlanta, GA: The Evaluation Working Group of the Centers for Disease Control and Prevention. Retrieved October 25, 2007, from http://www.cdc.gov/eval/resources.htm#logic%20model

Jung, B. C. (2007). *Evaluation resources on the Internet.* Retrieved October 25, 2007, from http://www.bettycjung.net/Evaluation.htm

For logic model development toolkits, see:

Enhancing program performance with logic models. (n.d.). Madison: University of Wisconsin Cooperative Extension Service. Retrieved October 25, 2007, from http://www.uwex.edu/ces/lmcourse/

Graig, E. (n.d.). *Logic models: A tutorial.* Useable Knowledge, LLC. Retrieved October 25, 2007, from http://www.usablellc.net/Logic%20Model%20(Online)/Presentation_Files/index.html

Point K: Practical tools for planning, evaluation and action—Logic model builder. (n.d.). Washington, DC: Innovation Network. Retrieved October 25, 2007, from http://www.innonet.org/index.php?section_id=64&content_id=185

Community toolbox: Developing a theory of change or logic model. (n.d.). Lawrence: University of Kansas. Retrieved October 2007, from http://ctb.ku.edu/tools/en/section_1877.htm

For logic model development software, see:

Logic model. (n.d.). Toronto: Performancesoft, Inc. Retrieved October 25, 2007, from http://www.performancesoft.com/solutions/logic-model/software.asp?Solution=plm

Outcome tracking software and outcomes-based applications. (n.d.). Durham, NC: Results Technologies Solutions, Inc. Retrieved October 25, 2007, from http://resultstechnologies.net/resources/primary_attributes.php

CHAPTER 4

Modeling

Improving Program Logic Models

This chapter focuses on improving models through simple processes that test feasibility. With careful and deliberate review, models for an idea, program, or project can change and mature in their quality. Logic models that are accurate and realistic representations of what you do and will get can increase the likelihood of effectiveness.

Learner Objectives

- Apply simple review and improvement steps to models
- Identify common errors in program logic models
- Recognize the value of multiple versions of models
- Recognize contributors to model quality

The process of modeling supports *better thinking* about a given idea or effort. It can establish routines wherein alternative possibilities are considered and explored. Modeling may be an important antidote to snap judgments. We see modeling as an essential step that has tremendous potential to position a project, program, or initiative for greater effectiveness. It generally involves several versions or attempts at models that result from a critical review of the information displayed.

Modeling and Effectiveness

Once a shared model is created, then those who created the model and others who are external to the program should spend time on its critique and revision. Great plans and programs come from great models. Great models require several rounds of revision. Modeling is the most important content in this book because improvement (rather than display) is what refines the content of the model. Modeling is a means to illustrate where you are headed, make better decisions about getting there, and get closer to the right work. We think it is important to test both plausibility and feasibility through modeling. In Chapter 2, we stated that plausibility is the most important criterion for a theory of change model. The process of toggling between combinations of strategies and results to secure an evidence-based model tests and verifies plausibility. We provide techniques that address the aspect of feasibility once plausibility has been established or confirmed. These criteria reflect the widely used *Program Evaluation Standards* (1994) that include utility, feasibility, propriety, and accuracy. Given the strong relationship between programming (strategy) and evaluation (results), we draw upon what constitutes sound evaluation practice to inform logic model development.

This chapter identifies some of the common context challenges that influence models and mitigate their potential. Some result in flaws embedded in the models and others occur in the modeling process. Our list includes blind spots, myths, "logic," and scale. We also name an overarching concern: culture. It can influence all the preceding items and more. Next, we identify some quality review techniques for program logic models. Through this sequence, we name the problems often associated with models and attempt to offer some remedies.

Context Challenges

Common Pitfalls: Blind Spots and Myths

Generating high-quality models through modeling is not easy, but both the products and the process do offer significant benefits. Some discomfort among participants during modeling can be an indicator that the process is useful. This discomfort probably reflects the twists, turns, flips, and angles of new or different thinking. It is important to be aware of blind spots (which we all have). Individuals have blind spots and small groups can have collective ones they protect and promote through interaction among participants. Blind spots are simply unintentional omissions in our thinking or commissions of error that happen because of habit (e.g., snap judgments, confidence, experience enables them). Eventually, these blind spots show up in our models because models represent current maps of how we think.

Prevailing myths are another pitfall to guard against. Common examples of myths include "access equals use, knowledge equals action, activities equals outcomes" and "send equals communication." These "myths" end up as embedded flaws in models because they are not precisely named and subsequently discarded. Almost every organization, department, or unit perpetuates some myths. We think it's how people defend and rationalize bad habits. These habits are often a way of coping with the organization, a boss, a funder, or other entity. Avoiding the pitfalls of blind spots and myths through disciplined and intentional discovery can contribute to model quality and eventually to program effectiveness.

Logic, Scale, and Specificity

Logic models often display a logical sequence or chain of events, but this is not the same as feasibility. The content and order of activities as well as other elements in a model can make sense, but scale is often an obstacle. Scale is about the relative size of a given effort. In particular, we mean the relationship between the results sought and the quality, volume, frequency, and other characteristics of the intervention or "doing" that is described.

For example, a logic model could name "a just, sustainable community" as its impact. Strategies to secure that intention might include some nonprofit capacity development and leadership development. It is logical to think these strategies might eventually contribute to a just, sustainable community. But, these strategies alone are insufficient to achieve the desired impact. There are other essential strategies necessary for this recipe to yield "justice and sustainability." This theory of change model is not plausible.

Subsequently, as activities are selected (in association with the capacity and leadership development strategies), they are far too dilute to have influence. A program, if deployed as described, would be unable to make progress against such an ambitious impact. This is particularly true given the 3 to 5 years allotted to most grant-funded programs to secure results (outcomes and impact). Engaging a few leaders and nonprofit organizations is inadequate to the huge ambition of a just, sustainable community given the enormous number of variables that can intervene. The program logic is not feasible.

If the scale of effort does not match short-term outcomes, then its relative paucity can overwhelm chances of success. (It is best to revise the model and indicate something that is appropriate, given limitations.) The first error in plausibility is compounded by a second error of feasibility. This example illustrates why logic, alone, is not an adequate quality test for models. It is important to note that sometimes theory of change models are plausible although the program logic model is not feasible. We believe success is more likely when plausibility and feasibility are evident in both models.

Given limited human and financial resources along with a time frame, it's important to specify your program or change initiative carefully. Making these choices is difficult but very important. We applaud audacious and substantial change agendas. However, success is more likely secured if your work is discrete and seeks near-term outcomes that, if accomplished, will contribute to results. For example, consider ending childhood obesity. This is an important and big result that reflects a complex systems challenge. Rather than taking on all of this substantial responsibility, perhaps the program effort that reflects your niche is focused on a single aspect such as more physically active middle school children. A reduction in childhood obesity will be more likely if you describe a selected population of children, their gender, their school district, and details of the activities that will constitute your project. These choices focus your results and intended outcomes. They also help inform the best prescription to deliver the dose needed to secure success. We know from experience that specificity is linked to success. Specificity does not preclude scale or ambition; it can complement those issues. We suggest that efforts with limited resources and/or relatively short time horizons be focused on outcomes that are earlier in the sequence on the path to the vision of the future you want to create. These more proximal outcomes can help define a contribution to the desired results. The strength of logic models lies in articulating the contribution to desired impact.

Probability statistics underscores our point: with fewer variables, the likelihood of the optimal combination increases. As the variables increase in number, the likelihood of success declines. We advocate for "smaller bites." It simply means picking which results are likely and moving backward from those results while employing a feasibility lens to determine the activities needed to develop plans, programs, or related efforts.

Politics, Persuasion, and Perception

Sometimes errors in scale are an authentic oversight. Other times, the politics of context are the origin. It is quite common for agendas that include marketing or positioning to supersede what's feasible. Models can be very persuasive. Something that is simple and clearly described in a graphic format is compelling. Models often help to persuade others because they clarify meaning and provide a logical organizer consistent with how people think, from actions to consequence. Depending on intended use, beware of models that are vague, general, and lack focus. Grandiose hyperbole in a model can indicate it is a marketing tool. Because logic models are socially constructed, it is important to beware that they may represent a shared view—but not necessarily factual truth or reality. The model can display "the" truth or perception of those who created it—or a combination of both. It is an error to assume every model is an evidenced-based prescription. The rigor of models in this matter varies considerably and reflects the context of their purpose and construction.

We indicated early in the book that models are co-created to ensure shared meaning. Exchange with and among participants during the model creation and modeling helps to generate common language. This process also ensures a display that is both intentional and commonly understood. A model that conveys consistent messages among those who created it may not have the same meaning to others because they missed the dialogue, exchange, and iterative processes. An important challenge in this group work is avoiding simple compromise. Compromise may satisfy the intra-group dynamics and politics, but it is not the same as strategy. Models need to reflect strategic thinking and choices. Keeping the focus on strategic choices to secure the intended end results are crucial to model quality and ultimately to program effectiveness.

Besides feasibility, we think program logic models should aim at utility. For this reason alone models will look different depending on the co-creators and the intended model use. This situational aspect applies to the level of detail in a given model, too. Program logic models can be complete but vary considerably in their content. What one group determines as a useful level of detail may be inadequate for another. Others may choose to model certain aspects of their program with different level of detail. Chapters 6 and 7 display some of this variance in format and use in case profiles and examples. The social construction of models means they will inevitably reflect assumptions, expectations, use, and other context features.

A Learning Culture and External Review

How models are created influences their format and content. We've already mentioned the composition of the review group. In addition, the culture (norms, values, beliefs) of those gathered to create and/or improve the model is very important. The best culture for improving models is one focused on learning from experience. This implies lots of variation in and versions of models that will help secure the one (eventually) used for plans and execution. Mistakes are critical to learning and it's important that "mistakes" are welcomed. People often need the subjective processes of critical review to identify errors and eventually secure remedies. Nobody draws a "perfect" model on his or her initial attempt. We believe a perfect model is not attainable regardless of the number of attempts. Any model simply represents a snapshot of the best thinking at a given point in time.

Processes to test logic models can retain and engage the original stakeholders who first drafted it. However, models improve most dramatically when introduced to colleagues or external sources that are not directly invested in the models' elements or their implementation. In this way, "disinvested" parties can offer objective critiques which often uncover blind spots, identify weaknesses, flaws, leaps of faith, ambiguities, "cockamamie," and fiction.

When inviting an external review, it's important to be aware that people may see and read models differently than those who created them. An external review can help provide great insight to both improved model content (e.g., resources, activities, outputs) and relative display (by virtue of placement and arrows that indicate relationship among content). Moving from general to specific, ask those doing an external review a series of questions. For example, initial questions might discover more about how the parts fit or do not fit together, what are other ways the same results could be achieved, and if the resources are adequate? The review might also inquire about the assumptions embedded in the model. And ask about the underlying theory of change it has been built upon.

Quality Techniques

Modeling

Most ideas, projects or programs can be characterized in their "life" to include four simple stages: design, implementation, evaluation, adaptation. We suggest that modeling is most useful when done in the creation stage and during evaluation, but models can be used at any stage for different purposes. Getting things right at the start can be very important to ultimate results and is a key influence to subsequent stages. Modeling can be thought of as a review process that occurs prior to implementation or execution. It is done to improve thinking and the models which reflect thinking. Time and effort spent in this work can have enormous return on investment, through the influence on the program itself. The steps in modeling are draw and test. This construct is displayed in Figure 4.1.

As a program, project, or idea is created, we suggest it gets drawn as a model. The "draw" step is satisfied when all elements of a program model (see Chapter 3) are present. Completion of this step means resources, activities, outputs, outcomes, and impact are named. This provides an opportunity to graphically display the thinking behind how the ideas framed in the theory of change will be implemented as a program. Many efforts with logic models quit at this point. However, through modeling, you can move quickly to dialogue to process the content and the "tangles." Tangles represent areas of confusion or where some in your group think a choice is wrong, confusing, or poorly specified. Modeling is the process that guides model improvement.

In this chapter, we begin to name how and what can test (or explore) model quality. We believe this testing can help improve models. The subsequent versions of models, which results from literal and figurative "tests" are products of modeling. This process can yield benefits to the specific idea or project as well as the individuals engaged as a work group. It is important to be aware that many external issues influence modeling. We describe some of those issues, but our list is not exhaustive.

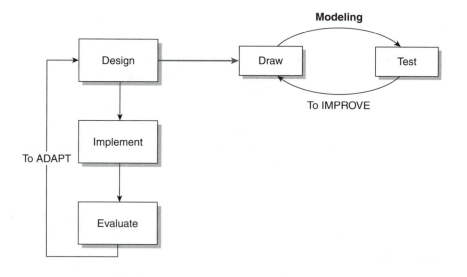

Figure 4.1   Relationship of Modeling to Program Life Cycle

Testing Model Quality: SMART and FIT

In a conscious testing effort, one way to explore the quality of a model is to apply SMART principles to it. SMART, as we use it in our practice, is an acronym for:

Specific: what to do is clear enough to act on and is connected to outcomes.

Measurable: the content can be both quantified and qualified.

Action oriented: the content is selected to provoke change in awareness, knowledge, skill, and/or behavior.

Realistic: the content is both plausible and feasible.

Timed: the content specifies a duration and illustrates the time-dependent sequence of outcomes for progress toward results.

If just a few people apply SMART principles to the outcomes portion of a program logic model, it will probably surface several flaws and, at the very least, some good questions. It may raise also concerns which are unique reflections of the training, experience, perspectives, and style among those contributing to the review. We suggest that a SMART analysis be applied to both parts and the whole. In other words, it can be used to examine selected individual strategy strands, activities, as well as the model as a comprehensive effort.

A second way to explore or test the quality of a model is to consider FIT. FIT is an acronym. It stands for:

Frequency of occurrence,

Intensity or strength of the given effort,

Targeted at a specified market or audience.

FIT principles offer an easy way to consider the process elements of the program, project or idea you display in your model. They translate to important questions about the adequacy of dose relative to intended results. The frequency reference implies this question: Does the project (idea or program) repeat, occur with appropriate volume, or happen often enough so that results are likely? The intensity reference implies this question: Does the project (idea or program) have enough depth or concentration that results are likely? The target reference implies this question: Does the project (idea or program) aim at an appropriate and specific audience or market segment?

In effect, FIT can remedy "treatment trickle." One thing known about resolution of problems or generating a change in awareness, knowledge, skill or behavior: the treatment (or intervention) needs to be both appropriate (the right choice) and adequate (the right dose). The wrong choice won't help get the results you want. The right choice has more chance of securing results but there needs to be enough of it (volume) focused on appropriate targets to ensure results. "Treatment trickle" means that a problem or challenge is under-dosed or an effort that is too broad or diluted to have impact. Feasibility is enhanced when we tackle a desired change with the right strategies/ activities as well as appropriate depth of intervention. Treatment trickle is common because people prefer to give everything or everyone "some," rather than make hard choices about who or what gets enough! It is often a reflection of limited resources, vague goals or organizations with an activities focus.

A "Mark Up"

In Figure 4.2, we revisit the logic model introduced in Chapter 1 for the Community Leadership Academy program. We suggest a technique that's often used in the legislative process as working drafts of language for a regulation or authorization are generated. It is called a "mark up." We adapt the legislative mark up, to raise important questions about model quality by applying SMART and FIT principles. Other elements, including context and technique questions can also be used. This discovery is aimed at changing the model in constructive ways that reflect evidence, strategic choices and better thinking. Using a disciplined approach to modeling captures an important opportunity for models to mature in quality.

Frequently, those who participate in developing a model judge how well it addresses the SMART and FIT criteria differently from how it is assessed by an external audience. This is because external reviewers may lack the context and shared meaning that emerge during development. Not all the meaning in a model is explicitly captured, displayed, or explained. The degree to which a model is SMART or FIT is highly contextual and situational. Ratings will depend on who the model is developed for, the model's purpose, and the level of detail the model is

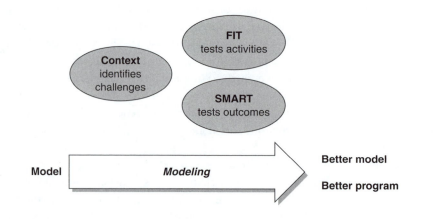

Figure 4.2   Modeling as Quality Review

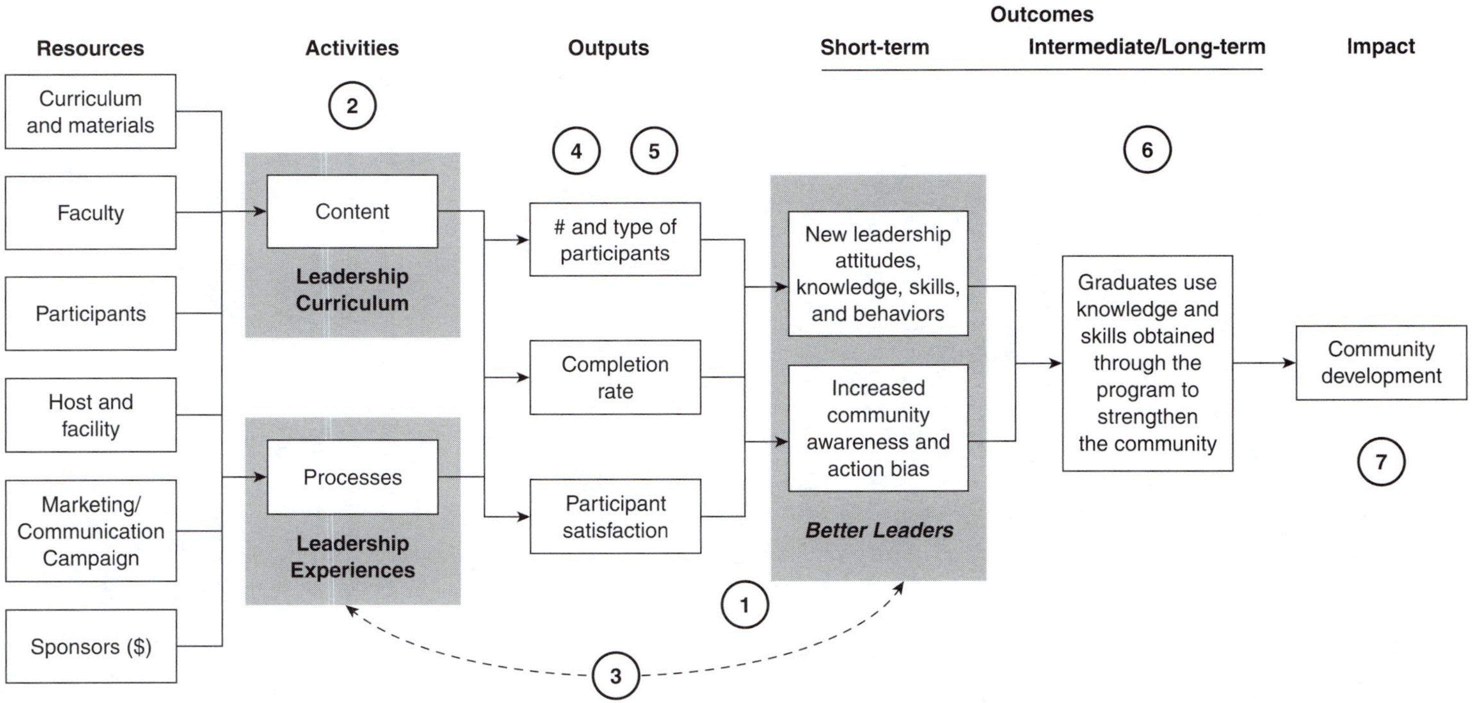
Outcomes
Resources
Activities
Outputs
Short-term
Intermediate/Long-term
Impact
Curriculum and materials
Faculty
Participants
Host and facility
Marketing/ Communication Campaign
Sponsors ($)
2
Content
Leadership Curriculum
Processes
Leadership Experiences
4
5
and type of participants
Completion rate
Participant satisfaction
New leadership attitudes, knowledge, skills, and behaviors
Increased community awareness and action bias
Better Leaders
1
3
6
Graduates use knowledge and skills obtained through the program to strengthen the community
Community development
7

Context

(1) This model emphasizes the academy perspective to what extent was the "community" involved in developing it?

(2) What leadership and/or community development theories inform the choices about curriculum and experiences?

(3) Does it make sense that the activities identified will contribute to the outcomes specified? Is the program, as illustrated feasible?

FIT

(4) How often does the academy meet? How long are the sessions? Over what period? Dose is important and should be included in the outputs.

(5) Who are the participants targeted by this program? How important is it to monitor recruitment and promotion activities? Neither are shown.

SMART

(6) The short- and intermediate/long-term outcomes are specific, measurable and action-oriented. The impact is not.

(7) What level of budget is needed/available to support the achievement of these outcomes? How long is reasonable to expect that it will take to see progress toward outcomes?

What about impact? How far out is this?

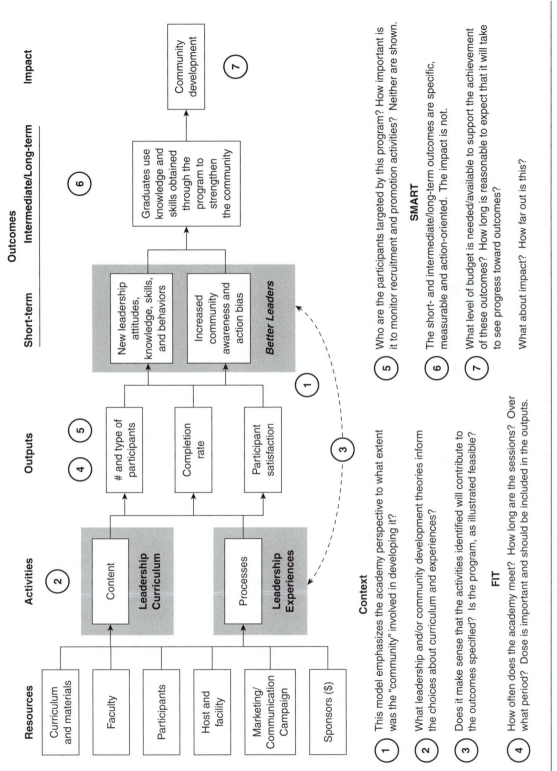

Figure 4.3 Community Leadership Academy Program Logic Model Mark Up

intended to communicate. If it is important that your model be self-explanatory under all conditions and/or viewed as credible to a wide variety of external audiences, then consider supplemental narrative. Remember, the model is a summary; it is usually not intended to tell the whole story.

In the Figure 4.3, questions generated from the application of SMART, FIT, and other process principles are placed on the model for discussion and resolution. The provoking dialogue that will likely occur will in turn result in changes to the model content based on new understandings, evidence and other contributions. Your review of this model may raise different questions about its feasibility.

Figure 4.4 uses the same mark up process to identify questions and concerns about content in the health model. As a constructive effort to critique and refine, quality testing is an important but often overlooked step.

In both of these mark ups, FIT questions aim primarily at the quality of process or intervention dose. SMART questions are focused on the feasibility of outcomes. It is easy to see that as the model increases in complexity the challenges to success increase, too. In a comprehensive effort, more pieces or parts must align and work together to secure the intended impact. The real time and context between activities and outcomes means many external issues also have the potential to influence the outcomes.

Typically, groups vary on how much emphasis they place on each of the characteristics of quality models described here. As with model interpretation and review, context and composition of the group frequently determine how the difficult distinction is made.

This also points to crucial issues in execution. When a model (representing an idea, project, or program) is evidence based, strategic, and well designed, implementation can still fail its potential. Although logic models are often used to inform evaluation, modeling at this stage is rarely done (see Chapter 5). Although outside the scope of this text, great execution is absolutely essential to results.

Quality Questions

The models you (and your colleagues) build reflect your collective thinking. Nobody would argue with this assumption: best thinking is a critical input to any work and its likely success. As you consider the design or plans for your project (program or idea) the following questions reflect quality considerations. They include application of the SMART and FIT principles. You might construct other questions based on your own experience or particular subject matter expertise. Think about ways to conduct discovery around blind spots, myths and other culture concerns. Regardless, it is important that deliberate efforts are invested in the maturation of a model. Modeling provides an opportunity to test, improve, and revise models. This process helps develop the thinking and the program that the model represents.

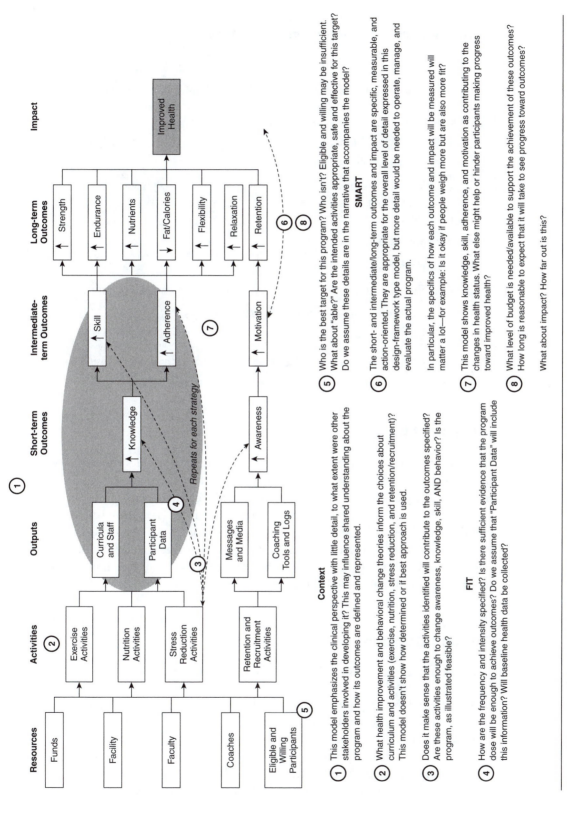

Resources

Funds

Facility

Faculty

Coaches

Eligible and Willing Participants ⑤

Activities ②

Exercise Activities

Nutrition Activities

Stress Reduction Activities

Retention and Recruitment Activities

Outputs

Curricula and Staff

Participant Data

Messages and Media

Coaching Tools and Logs

④

③

Repeats for each strategy

Short-term Outcomes ①

Knowledge

Awareness

Intermediate-term Outcomes

Skill

Adherence

⑦

Motivation

Long-term Outcomes

Strength

Endurance

Nutrients

Fat/Calories

Flexibility

Relaxation

Retention

⑥

⑧

Impact

Improved Health

Context

① This model emphasizes the clinical perspective with little detail, to what extent were other stakeholders involved in developing it? This may influence shared understanding about the program and how its outcomes are defined and represented.

② What health improvement and behavioral change theories inform the choices about curriculum and activities (exercise, nutrition, stress reduction, and retention/recruitment)? This model doesn't show how determined or if best approach is used.

③ Does it make sense that the activities identified will contribute to the outcomes specified? Are these activities enough to change awareness, knowledge, skill, AND behavior? Is the program, as illustrated feasible?

FIT

④ How are the frequency and intensity specified? Is there sufficient evidence that the program dose will be enough to achieve outcomes? Do we assume that "Participant Data" will include this information? Will baseline health data be collected?

⑤ Who is the best target for this program? Who isn't? Eligible and willing may be insufficient. What about "able?" Are the intended activities appropriate, safe and effective for this target? Do we assume these details are in the narrative that accompanies the model?

SMART

⑥ The short- and intermediate/long-term outcomes and impact are specific, measurable, and action-oriented. They are appropriate for the overall level of detail expressed in this design-framework type model, but more detail would be needed to operate, manage, and evaluate the actual program.

In particular, the specifics of how each outcome and impact will be measured will matter a lot—for example: Is it okay if people weigh more but are also more fit?

⑦ This model shows knowledge, skill, adherence, and motivation as contributing to the changes in health status. What else might help or hinder participants making progress toward improved health?

⑧ What level of budget is needed/available to support the achievement of these outcomes? How long is reasonable to expect that it will take to see progress toward outcomes?

What about impact? How far out is this?

Figure 4.4   Health Improvement Program Logic Model Mark Up

Quality Questions for Program Logic Models

1. Are the results specified with shared meaning among all stakeholders?

2. What research, practice, and theory are grounding for our choices in activities? Is there a relationship between the program logic model and a theory of change?

3. Did we challenge the recipe of activities and outcomes to ensure feasibility given the challenges we seek to resolve?

4. What activities have worked under similar conditions? What current conditions might influence selection of activities? Is there evidence that these activities are best?

5. Is the model FIT?

6. Are target audiences clearly defined?

7. Does the interaction among activities contribute to intended outcomes?

8. Do the outcomes feasibly contribute to intended results?

9. Is the model SMART?

10. Do we have adequate resources and time to accomplish intended results?

A Quality Model

Figure 4.5 displays characteristics for model quality. It assembles key narrative from this chapter into a graphic. The figure describes two important standards for model quality: plausibility and feasibility. The quality characteristics for theory of change models are noted (as in Chapter 2), where the focus is on the relationship between strategies and results. The quality characteristics for a program logic model are captured by FIT and SMART principles. We suggest the application of this in a "mark up" is one way to work with colleagues in modeling. We think, taken together, theory of change models that are plausible and program logic models that are feasible can contribute to effectiveness.

"Better" Decisions

Earlier in the text, we asked three questions about effectiveness:

- Are you doing the right work?
- Can you make better decisions?
- Are you getting superior results?

The second, about making "better decisions" is highly central to modeling. In effect, we apply this query to strategy and activity selection relative to results. How

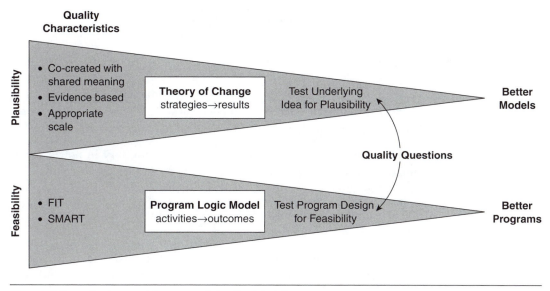

Figure 4.5   Factors and Features of Quality Models

you choose to focus time, energy, talents and resources in relation to your specified success is related directly to effectiveness. There are many ways to secure a named intention. Discarding strategies/activities which are peripheral, modest contributors or less than optimal focus limited resources. Further, specificity about strategies and activities contribute to the results you and your colleagues intend to secure. Ambiguity should be avoided. Eventually, "right work" is also about the strategies and activities in the program logic model. Giving conscious attention to the criterion employed in selecting strategies for the theory of change model and then, the specific activities in the program logic model can make a big difference in securing results. "Right work" gets clarified and better decisions considered through the process of modeling. Models and their versions can develop discipline as well as standard practices which contribute to new understandings about what will generate progress on results.

In Summary

Although frequently overlooked, modeling is a helpful technique to improve your chances of success because great design and plans come from great models. We suggest iterative versions of models are co-created through a disciplined process that tests and retests quality. Models can be greatly influenced by unintentional omissions (blind spots), myths, politics, persuasions, and perceptions. Logic, scale, and specificity all have a bearing on models, too. A simple way to explore model quality is the application of SMART and FIT principles. We suggest a "mark up" as a good way to critically review your program logic model.

Learning Resources

Reflection

1. Given how subjective PLMs are, what are the implications for the outside "reader" of a model? What does a model that will be "read" and perhaps used by those other than those who constructed it have to communicate?

2. What role might politics, persuasion, or perception play in how a model might be created, tested, and improved? How do these issues influence model quality and use?

3. What prevailing myths might influence choices in your workplace or family? How do blind spots influence choices?

4. How might the improvement process for a simple, single site project model be different from that for a more complex multi-site, multi-level initiative? What concerns should the model development team be sure to address and what aspects of the model will be most important to communicate?

5. Can a complex, comprehensive program be effectively modeled with a single diagram? Why or why not? How would you approach a task like this?

Exercises

1. Imagine what a strand focused on marketing might look like to promote an innovative new hearing aid. Make an assignment for individuals to illustrate this strand. Give them all the same amount of specified financial resources over 12 months and tell them the desired outcome is maximum sales volume. Then, ask them to name their target market, key activities in the marketing strategy. Compare and contrast versions each participant creates. What assumptions, knowledge, or evidence accounts for the differences in how the marketing strands are constructed? What criteria is useful to reconcile these different illustrations?

2. Consider the questions raised in Figure 4.3 about the Community Leadership Academy Program Logic Model. How would you answer them? What would the model look like once those questions had your answers? Draw it and discuss the implications of your response to the mark up.

   Consider the questions raised in Figure 4.4 about the Health Improvement Program. How would you answer them? What would the model look like once those questions had your answers? Draw it and discuss the implications of your response to the mark up.

3. Draw a logic model for learning a foreign language. Ask a colleague to conduct a mark up using SMART and FIT on the models. What might change? How? Why?

References and Supplemental Readings

Texts

The Joint Committee on Standards for Educational Evaluation. (1994). *The program evaluation standards: How to assess evaluations of educational programs* (2nd ed.). Thousand Oaks, CA: Sage.

Van Hecke, M. L. (2007). *Blind spots: Why smart people do dumb things.* Amherst, NY: Prometheus.

Journal Articles

Alter, C., & Egan, M. (1997). Logic modeling: A tool for teaching critical thinking in social work practice. *Journal of Social Work Education, 33*(1).

Dwyer, J. (1996). Applying program logic model in program planning and evaluation. *Public Health and Epidemiology Report Ontario, 7*(2), 38–46.

Julian, D. (1997). The utilization of the logic model as a system level planning and evaluation device. *Evaluation and Program Planning, 20*(3), 251–257.

Renger, R. (2006). Consequences to federal programs when the logic-modeling process is not followed with fidelity. *American Journal of Evaluation, (27)*12, 452–463.

Rush, B., & Ogbourne A. (1991). Program logic models: expanding their role and structure for program planning and evaluation. *Canadian Journal of Program Evaluation, 6,* 95–106.

Internet Resources

In addition to practicing the review steps on your own models, there are many other examples of logic models to work from available on the Internet. For two different approaches, see:

Logic models. (n.d.). Tucson: University of Arizona Cooperative Extension. Retrieved October 25, 2007, from http://ag.arizona.edu/extension/pda/logicmodel/index.html

Capable communities: Examples. (n.d.). East Lansing: Michigan State University. Retrieved October 25, 2007, from http://outreach.msu.edu/capablecommunities/examples.asp

PART II

Applications

CHAPTER 5

Logic Models for Evaluation Literacy

This chapter focuses on using logic models as the architecture for deeper engagement of stakeholders in discussion about evaluation design. Logic models inform the development of several elements of evaluation design. Logic models are powerful even if they have not been used for program planning. This chapter covers selected concepts useful to an evaluation consumer.

Learner Objectives

- Describe the contributions logic models can make to evaluation design
- Use a logic model to focus on evaluation information needs
- Use a logic model to provoke dialogue on both process and results indicators
- Identify how logic models can be used to inform effectiveness

Getting More Out of Evaluation

Connecting Management With Measurement

So far, logic models in Chapters 2 through 4 have been shown as significant tools to assist in improving the thinking behind the design and/or planning of your efforts. At this point, remember that the model is just an illustration. A model at the program planning stage functions much like the map an explorer would use to guide a journey—to chart new direction. It highlights the portions of program operations as well as the pathways and milestones you believe are most critical to achieving desired results. The assumptions that were used to construct the model during program planning need to be put to the test. As your program is implemented, there are ample opportunities to observe and collect information about what works and what does not. Evaluation, whether informal and anecdotal or formal and highly technical, supplies that vital information.

Evaluation is not just performed by evaluators. All day long, people determine (and use) information about processes and connect it to results. They do this to assess progress and for the purpose of improvement. We all have at least once in our lives looked in the mirror, gasped, and made some adjustment, either right then or at some future point. In this situation, the result could be how we or others perceive our image. The process would be any of those actions we take to achieve the image we desire (haircut, wardrobe, grooming, etc). Any change in our actual appearance will be reflected in the mirror. Evaluation in isolation will not improve effectiveness—it is just an activity.

Funders, program staff, and participants are typically referred to in evaluation circles as stakeholders. We use this term in earlier chapters when explaining their role in logic model development during program planning. During program design, funders and program staff serve as the program architects and content experts, with participants as the experts in community context and benefit. However, when the time comes to use logic models for evaluation, the stakeholder role changes somewhat. During evaluation, stakeholders also play a key role as information users although they are not often experts at evaluation. This is why we refer to them as evaluation consumers in this chapter. Evaluation must be understood, appreciated, and used by evaluation consumers if it is to have any influence on improvement. It is only when evaluation consumers take a more active role in connecting what they do with what they get that they can benefit from their evaluation investment.

The logic model serves as the focal point for discussion about evaluation because it displays when, where, and how to look for the information most needed to manage the program and determine its effectiveness. Although this chapter focuses on using logic models to inform evaluation design, they can be used in a number of other ways to benefit programs as well. Because logic models show the key elements of your program, they can also be employed for focusing your internal communication or external dissemination messages, audiences, and products. In addition, logic models point out the categories of data sources, expertise, and documents essential to include when developing knowledge management systems to support program operations.

When the model of your program is used to guide evaluation it then becomes more of a navigational aid (informs direction) and dashboard (informs data collection and gauges progress). The crucial step in improving effectiveness, however, is to ensure the evaluation provides appropriate and timely feedback to management. It follows then that management is sufficiently evaluation literate and takes the time to reflect on the meaning and significance of evaluation data. For evaluation to be truly useful, its findings must be relevant, understood, and applied by program staff. Logic modeling enables evaluators, program staff, and funders to develop shared understanding about what the evaluation will cover, its purposes, and how the information collected will be used. The way to get more out of evaluation is to plan for its use right from the beginning.

Evaluation typically includes the collection, analysis, interpretation, and reporting of data needed to inform the decisions of those who fund, provide, or administer programs. Anytime assessment occurs, there is opportunity to apply the information gathered to improve the effectiveness of programs, policies, personnel, products, and organizations. We believe that one key to effectiveness is to couple program design and implementation *with* evaluation. Logic models help accomplish this because they provide a set of clear, measurable, and realistic program processes and outcomes. If these are overly optimistic or are not measurable, the program may neither be able to operate as planned *nor* demonstrate that it has been effective.

A decade ago, logic models were used almost exclusively to plan and execute evaluations. Over time, evaluators and program staff have learned that there are benefits to building the evaluative thinking that the logic model process brings right from the start. A logic model for evaluation is like the "bookend" or mirror image of one for planning and implementation. They both display the same content. By using a logic model to inform evaluation design program staff, funders, and evaluators can have a clearer picture of what their evaluation will measure and produce.

This chapter does not prepare you to conduct an evaluation. Instead, it points out the key areas where a logic model can support program staff, funders, and evaluators during evaluation design. They do this by focusing decisions on what the evaluation will include and by planning for the use of evaluation information to support learning and program improvement. This chapter shows how the architecture of logic models can be used as the platform to guide discussions about for whom, why, where, and when evaluation activities should occur to generate maximum utility. Through evaluative thinking and enhanced awareness about evaluation, models can support a more active role for program staff and funders in shaping evaluation to better meet their learning and accountability needs.

Evaluation for Effectiveness

In simple terms, evaluation often involves a critical review of the strategies and activities (the "doing") selected, and their implementation and results (the "getting"). There are two basic types of evaluation: summative and formative evaluation. The following metaphor is widely used to illustrate the difference between these two types of evaluation. When the cook tastes the soup, that is formative evaluation, but when the guests taste the soup, that is summative evaluation.

A summative evaluation is typically done for the purpose of accountability and determines whether intended results were achieved. It generally responds to the question: What difference did we make? So this type tends to emphasize the "getting" or outcomes and impact side of the model. Summative evaluation tends to be retrospective in that it usually occurs at the conclusion of a program. For example, the summative evaluation of an educational initiative might focus solely on student achievement. Or a summative policy evaluation might look only for changes in specific legislation.

A formative evaluation is most often used for the purposes of learning about what works and/or program improvement. It generally responds to the question: How can we be more effective? Formative evaluation focuses prospectively on improvement by looking at both the "doing" and the "getting" side of the model. It looks at the relationship or "logical" connection between processes and outcomes throughout the program duration. Building on the educational initiative example above, a formative evaluation might also examine and address the quality of instruction, curriculum, and/or assessment. Similarly, a formative policy evaluation might examine the quality of the policy maker education efforts and look for changes in attitudes or knowledge as essential first steps toward legislative action. Evaluation findings might show program leadership and staff that their message is not persuasive enough, that their contact is too brief, or that too few policy makers are reached and might suggest that they change their approach accordingly.

These two types are complementary but the lines of distinction between the two are often highly contextual and blurred. The information both approaches can produce is needed to improve results. Regrettably, most evaluations are conducted for compliance with requirements set by funding sources, including governments and grantmakers. Many times, such evaluations are not used by program managers, funders, or other stakeholders. Typically, these evaluations are focused on verification that dollars were spent in approved categories and that target audiences received services in the numbers anticipated; very little focus is on the difference made. So, these evaluations often capture and codify information already known by the program staff. Sometimes they are highly technical, academic, and explore aspects that have little relevance to the day-to-day operation of a specific program.

Improved effectiveness requires that evaluation consumers have the information they need. Achieving that requires some degree of engagement by evaluation consumers in the evaluation design process. Logic models facilitate communication between evaluation experts and the consumers they serve. They communicate the essence of a program as envisioned to inform evaluation. Conversely, they also communicate the essence of the evaluation to inform program.

Evaluation Design Basics

Where Consumers Add Value

Typically, evaluators rely on an evaluation plan to communicate the details of what they propose to do. Evaluation consumers frequently use the evaluation plan as the starting point for evaluation contracting. An evaluation plan should describe what information it will secure, what purpose it will serve, and for whom. In addition, it often includes methods for data collection, a schedule for tasks (or a timeline), personnel qualifications, reporting, and cost. There is often quite a bit of negotiation from the original request for proposals, initial proposal, and final evaluation plan. It is during this back and forth between the evaluation experts and consumers that evaluation-literate consumers can best take action to focus their evaluation investment on effectiveness. Readers interested in detailed information on evaluation are referred to the Supplemental Readings list at the end of this chapter.

Figure 5.1 shows the basic elements of an evaluation design. Reading from left to right, an evaluation design first and foremost needs to specify the purpose of the evaluation. Purpose includes the intended use and who will use it. As you recall, formative evaluation serves program improvement and summative serves the purpose of accountability. However, both types of evaluation have the same design elements. After that, the design should describe the information needed to address the questions inferred by the expressed purpose. Next, the indicators that further specify the quality and quantity of information are developed. From the indicators, the range of methods and types of appropriate analyses can be determined. Indicators also inform the schedule and type of reporting because they show when data might be available and how best to communicate results.

This chapter is limited to information needs, questions, and indicators because this is where evaluation consumers are most able to add value. These three elements define the core content the evaluation needs to address if the evaluation is to be used as intended. Evaluation consumers are the program experts and can inform evaluation design in ways that keep the purpose the evaluation must serve in the forefront. With this focus, those charged with conducting the evaluation (whether external consultants or internal staff) are better able to select appropriate methods to capture pertinent information and work with consumers to agree on reporting style and timing. Those conducting the evaluation are counted on to provide methodological and communication expertise.

Evaluation has some of the same limitations that program design, planning, and implementation face: time, talent, and money. These limits mean that there are important choices to make relative to information needs and processes to secure information. Questions like the following become the foundation for evaluation design:

- What are the priority areas for inquiry?
- What are the key questions about those areas that we need to answer?
- What is "fair" to expect in outcomes given resources and effort in the program?
- What will be used as indicators of sufficient effort (process) and progress (outcomes)?

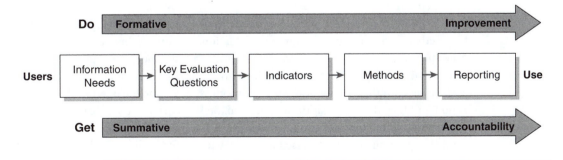

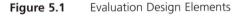

Figure 5.1   Evaluation Design Elements

The evaluation design process pursues answers to these (and other) questions. So, how does the use of logic models support evaluation consumers in advocating for their interests during design?

Where Logic Models Add Value

Because a logic model (whether a theory of change or a program model) illustrates the relationship between planned or actual work and results, it supports evaluation through commonly understood visual architecture. This architecture assists in the formulation of key questions and indicators about the program and its effects over time. It does this in ways that encourage evaluation use that targets improved effectiveness. Subsequently, appropriate data collection methods and other aspects of the full evaluation plan can be identified. All too often, groups are eager to rush into measurement without first determining what should be measured and why.

Because only limited resources are usually available for the evaluation, it is important to identify who the evaluation users are and determine what they *need* to know. Generally, there is lots of discussion about what they *want* to know or *could* know. Evaluations are rarely allocated resources that provide for a thorough examination of all program elements and their relationships as expressed in a model. Logic models and modeling (which display versions or aspects in greater detail) can help explore options and point to the most strategic choices for evaluation investment. Sometimes the evolution of an evaluation design is a long dance.

At the outset, clear determinations of users and their uses are important considerations. Knowing your audiences and their information needs will support good choices and focus your evaluation so that it has optimal utility. In practice, the functional objective is to specify what information is essential *and* secure an evaluation that discovers and delivers in response to that need. The logic model and modeling process provide the architecture against which evaluation experts and consumers can decide. The power of evaluation is harnessed when the findings and analysis generated are *applied* to the work examined. With logic models as the framework for design decisions, evaluation can provide critical feedback loops about the progress of a strategy, program, initiative, or organization toward its desired results.

Evaluation consumer participation in the logic model development process (whether during program planning, evaluation, or both) helps to ensure that the evaluation services they procure address their needs. The tools and processes of logic modeling provide the opportunity to build common language and understanding with their evaluation partners about what will be included in the evaluation and how the information will be used. Stakeholders, in the role of evaluation consumers, need to know enough about the evaluation design process to have input on the questions to be addressed and the evidence that will be used to determine success. Given that the logic model is the graphic representation of the program's key processes and outcomes, consumers can then easily identify and advocate for those aspects of the model most important from their perspective to manage and measure.

While the reasons and expectations for evaluation can vary, we are predisposed to utility. This requires a clear determination of who needs to know what about the program and to what end? Without logic models to portray a shared understanding of the evaluation, it may serve some or none of your audiences. For evaluation to make its full contribution to performance management and effectiveness, it is important to design the evaluation as a resource that can support the learning of those for whom its use is intended.

A Design Example

Two Kinds of Learning

We use theory of change *and* program logic models to plan programs and their evaluations because together they better stimulate conversations and subsequently learning about those aspects of a program most essential to success. One important concept frequently overlooked is that in order to use evaluation to improve effectiveness, you need to engage in learning.

Organizational learning and development experts often speak of two types of learning that are needed to improve program effectiveness. The first type of learning examines the current program and uses evaluation information to improve the program as it was originally envisioned. This type of learning, technically referred to as "single loop," does not question the assumptions and evidence that underlie the program design. The original thinking is a given and is not examined. This type of learning is focused on simple changes in the quality and quantity of activities directed toward producing increasingly better versions of what you originally intended. In this case, evaluation is used to test and improve the "logic" behind implementation. Effectiveness is improved incrementally.

The second type of learning examines whether the original program design is sound. This type of "double loop" learning can transform an effort into something dramatically different from what was initially intended. Here when activities do not seem to produce intended results, the strategies themselves or the likely outcomes may be questioned and altered. Evaluation that serves this type of learning is used to test the theory of change (connection between strategies and results) and improve the logic behind the design and/or model that drives implementation. For readers interested in more information about single and double loop learning, see the Supplemental Readings list provided at the end of this chapter.

In this section, we use the general Community Leadership Academy (CLA) program logic model example introduced earlier to show how models can be used to develop and communicate evaluation design that serve both types of learning.

Key Evaluation Questions

In Chapter 1, using the example of the CLA program, we introduced model types: theory of change, program, and evaluation. Before we review those models it is important to understand that key evaluation questions develop from simple questions. These questions are, "What did we do?" and "What did we get?" They are asked at the level of the theory of change for the program as shown in Figure 5.2. Evaluation helps us examine the links in the logic underneath the planned work and its connection to desired results. By this link, we mean "testing" whether or not the theory of change as originally modeled actually described what happened. Does the original thinking that asserted, "If we do X, Y, and Z, we will get the results we want," hold true? Here the model serves double loop learning by helping focus attention on the bigger picture. Before any effort is invested in improving the program as it is currently designed, the question of whether it was the "right" thing to do should be determined. By this, we mean two things. First, relative to goal attainment, we would ask, "Is it aligned with broader organizational goals?" Second, relative to the activities selected, "Were they among the best choices we could have made to achieve our desired ends?" This is particularly important in those instances where logic modeling was not used during program design.

The CLA theory of change model (Figure 5.2) helps us explore potential areas for focused discovery and learning. The basic "do" and "get" questions help to shape the information the evaluation can deliver. Recall, this program had two strategies: curriculum and experiences.

In the CLA example, key evaluation questions were co-constructed with the client, who sought external evaluation services. This client, a foundation, had sponsored the program for almost 20 years. It and other stakeholders wanted to know what difference this effort had made and ways the program could be improved. The program design is simple. It assumes participants (as an input) and provides greater detail about the two strategies named in the theory of change: leadership curricula and experiences. An obvious first question (see Figure 5.2) is whether or not leadership curriculum and experiences are the right strategies in a leadership program aimed at community development. It is important to focus evaluation on testing this basic assumption (or "link") about the "right work" because it is the foundation for the program design. Figure 1.3 shows this first question on the program logic model for the purposes of introductory explanation. Here, because it is "testing" at the strategy level, we place it on the theory of change.

It is also important to note that the CLA, as well as other projects, initiatives, and organizations, operates in a larger system. For the CLA, it is a specific community. Organizations operate in other layers of reality besides geography. This might be a sector or a country. These contexts certainly have issues, both barriers and facilitators that can exert tremendous influence on impact. In the CLA example, it may be the abundance or lack of participants. Or perhaps it is a culture reluctant to invite program graduates into community work. Organizations are subject to many other kinds of influences in their external environment, like labor practices, taxes, or consumer whims. It is worth mentioning here because sometimes evaluations aim at discovery relative to barriers and facilitators and these are not always specifically stated

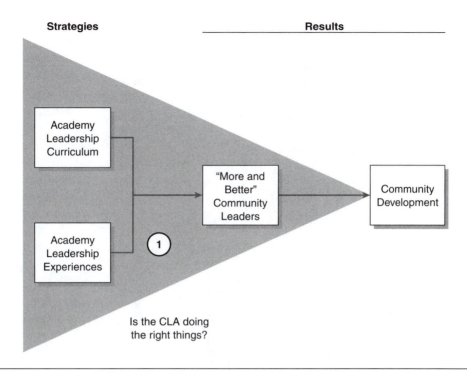

Strategies   **Results**

Academy Leadership Curriculum

Academy Leadership Experiences

①

"More and Better" Community Leaders

Community Development

Is the CLA doing the right things?

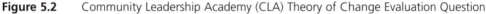

Figure 5.2   Community Leadership Academy (CLA) Theory of Change Evaluation Question

in a theory of change model. When it is possible to include the examination of these influences in evaluation, they can support improvement and/or help explain results.

In Figure 5.3, the program logic model is used to determine the other key questions central to evaluation design. In this display we indicate those key questions that test the implementation logic. This information can be used to determine areas for improvement and to increase the likelihood or magnitude of effect. The key questions are placed near links of logic (areas of the model) that specify where deeper discovery about implementation might yield relevant information. It is important to note that the questions about outcome and impact need to be addressed for both types of learning. Both theory of change and program logic models show the same information, just in different detail as well as for different purposes.

Ultimately, the evaluation design for the CLA addressed these five key questions:

1. Is the Academy doing the right things?

Question 1 is about the "recipe" for the program. It seeks information about program content (strategies as well as the resources, activities, and outputs). It attends to discovery about these, their interaction and contribution to results. This exact query is placed on the theory of change model (see Figure 5.2). The question is hidden in the program logic model where the program view has considerably more detail.

2. Is the Academy doing things right?

Question 2 is about the implementation quality or execution of the selected program content.

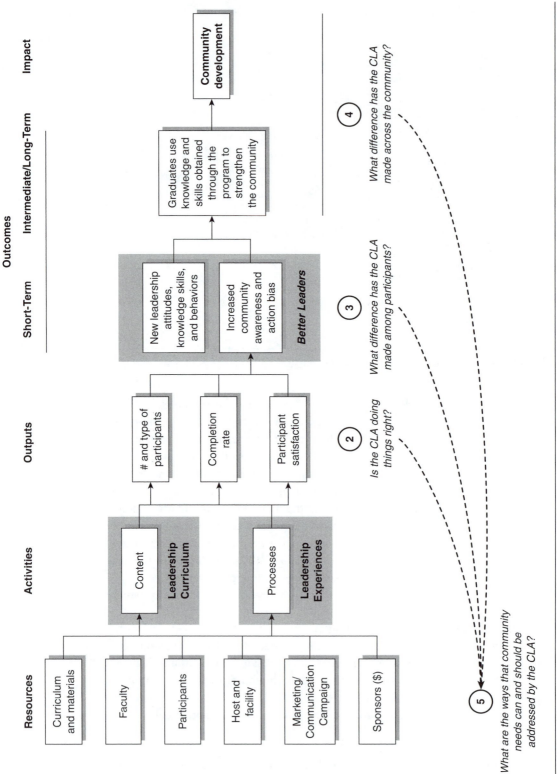

Figure 5.3   Community Leadership Academy Program Logic Model With Key Implementation Questions

3. **What difference has the Academy made for participants?**

Question 3 focuses on how individuals may have changed because of their Academy experience.

4. **What difference has the Academy made across the community?**

Question 4 examines the changes that could be attributed to the community because of the program.

5. **What are the different ways community needs can and should be addressed by the Academy?**

Question 5 seeks other information that can help inform a better or improved program. This might be by improving strategy and/or implementation.

These questions are *very typical* but highly general program evaluation questions. In some form, they may even have universal application because they represent common areas of interest about any program, project, or initiative. These questions can also be the basis for more precise inquiry or sub-questions in each area. Subsequently, data are collected to respond to questions.

Theory of change and program models for this effort share the same intended impact: "community development." Before evaluation and during planning, it could be useful to ensure shared understanding of what "community development" means and what it would look like if the program were successful. Does "community development" mean full employment, a vibrant arts culture, effective schools, all of these, or something else? Similarly, on the CLA theory of change model note that the outcome of "more, better leaders" precedes this desired impact. Assuming that "more and better" means an increased number of designated leaders with skills, then we could infer skill changes among Academy graduates. Arriving at shared understanding of what the terms used in the models actually mean helps determine how they can be measured.

The next place where evaluation consumers can provide insight into evaluation design is in the development of indicators. Program logic models, in particular, can be used to develop and display quite specific definitions of the evidence that evaluation experts and consumers agree is needed to "indicate" progress from strategy to results during implementation. To inform effectiveness, indicators of strategy and results are needed.

Indicators

We all need indicators to help us understand whether we are making progress. However, as most change does not occur instantly, it is important to have gauges that show progression over time. Indicators, when placed on the model, are the gauges that show how the program will demonstrate progress. An evaluation will typically focus primarily on the output and outcome elements when specifying indicators. Indicators are the evidence that will verify progress (or lack of) for a given output or outcome. Both kinds of indicators, outputs and outcomes, provide confirming or disconfirming information about progress toward impact. In this text, *process indicator* refers to those indicators selected to gauge progress against the outputs. The process indicators are the evidence you will collect to show what you "did." We use the term *outcome indicator* to distinguish those indicators of progress toward results (may include outcomes and impact). The outcome indicators are the evidence that you will collect to show what you "got."

For example, in a model about mine safety, you would need indicators of your efforts to achieve mine safety ("do," the process) and indicators that safety has been achieved ("get," the outcome). You might use a live (or dead canary) as an indicator of air quality (one of the many outputs needed to achieve mine safety). Here, the canary in a cage would be a process indicator. Alternatively, if we are focusing on mine safety as an outcome, accident reduction could be among the many outcome indicators selected. Similarly, if great hitters are important in winning baseball games, then batting averages are an output. Here, things like batting averages and type of hits would be process indicators. Games won would be an outcome indicator. In the text that follows, we will explain the concepts of process and outcome indicators using the CLA example. We take the CLA program logic model (Figure 5.3) and split it into process (Figure 5.4) and outcome (Figure 5.5) portions. In turn, we focus on the development of the more detailed process and then on outcome indicators needed to inform evaluation design.

On the program logic model, outputs serve as the indicators of whether or not the activities occurred as intended. For a program to achieve its intended results, it is important to have information about both the quantity and quality of the activities as well as the availability of resources to support the work. This is important because the concept of "dose" has a direct influence on effectiveness and your ability to improve your programs, if you think of your program as a treatment or intervention, much like a vaccination might be. How much of your program is actually delivered, who and how many participate, over what period of time, how "good" each activity is—all play a role in whether a program makes progress toward its intended outcomes and impact.

This information, if collected, can be used to monitor the program to ensure appropriate dose and to explain why progress toward desired results is or is not made. Outputs are concrete aspects of your program that you can adjust, as needed, to amplify your progress. The FIT acronym introduced earlier applies here as well. Establishing process indicators of the *f*requency (how often), *i*ntensity (quality and duration), and *t*argets (with whom) for your activities can go a long way to giving you the leverage you need to boost program performance. In the case of the policy example we used earlier, it is easy to see that a brochure left in the state house lunchroom is less likely to produce results than a series of lunchtime conversations, one-on-one with the key house leaders. The brochure is a relatively weak dose of policy maker education (i.e., single shot, indirect delivery, no follow-up) compared to a more comprehensive relationship building strategy.

When we apply these concepts to the activities in the CLA example, it is important to specify further the expected outputs. The following formative questions, applied to Figure 5.3, may prompt your thinking about this model. They can be tailored and used with groups to explore the process indicators for models you develop:

- What outputs would you expect or need to see from the curriculum?
- What outputs would you expect or need to see from experiences?
- What outputs must occur to support subsequent outcomes?

Figure 5.4 shows the range of process indicators the CLA evaluation identified as measures of the output or "dose" of the CLA curriculum and experience. Notice that they specify the quality of curriculum and experiences in addition to listing the

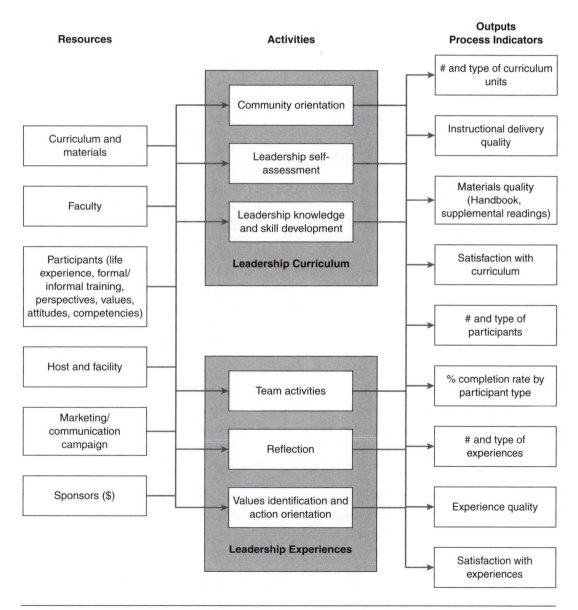

Figure 5.4   Community Leadership Academy Process Indicators

typical participant counts and satisfaction. Logic models used for evaluation typically display much more detailed information than those used during program design. Based on your thoughts about the questions above, what might be missing from this set of process indicators? What questions about implementation dose or fidelity might the CLA program not be able to address?

Recall that outcomes reflect the majority of the "getting" side of the logic model. Outcomes are also time sensitive. They occur in a typically fairly ordered sequence. This sequence or outcome chain illustrates the likely steps between "do" and "get." How tight or loose the order is will depend on the type of program being modeled. Sometimes the model might or might not show the specific connections from a given activity to each particular outcome. Some programs lend themselves to the description of distinct pathways from activities to outcomes while others are more holistic and show all activities leading to all outcomes. The degree to which interdependencies are strictly defined and clear entry points are predetermined can vary considerably. Most models represent a cluster of outcomes that occur at a number of levels (individuals, organizations, systems) from a combination of efforts. In any case, short-, intermediate-, and long-term outcomes inform evaluation design because they indicate when and where to look for evidence. This is particularly true when the program is very complex. What is likely to happen first, and then what? Sometimes the outcomes are sufficiently specified in the program logic model to guide measurement and other times the model needs to be adapted to serve evaluation design.

Developing evidence that would support your claims that an outcome has been achieved is among perhaps the most important steps in teasing out the specifics of your evaluation design. In individuals, changes in awareness, knowledge, skills, and behavior are a common, expected sequence of outcomes. In organizations or systems, the outcome sequence might include changes in context (the environment or external influences on the program), conditions (policies that govern practice, communication, and networks that spread it), and/or culture (relationships, norms and values). In some organizations, however, like those in public health, system and organizational changes are necessary precursors to change in behavior at the population level. It is important to understand and display these distinctions when developing models.

Turning our attention back to the CLA example, Figure 5.5 shows the set of initial outcome indicators identified for the CLA evaluation. Notice that the evaluation design does not state the community development impact with any specificity. The evaluation focused on short- and intermediate-term outcomes, in that these outcomes were more closely connected to the program itself as a training initiative as well as the limited budget and time frame available to conduct the evaluation. The CLA evaluation did not intend to test the theory of change beyond the contribution of its curriculum and experiences to more and better leaders. This level of specificity was sufficient to garner agreement from evaluation consumers on the broad categories of outcomes the evaluation would address. In addition, it is important to note how these outcomes meet the SMART criteria for outcomes described in earlier chapters. They are *s*pecific in that they name what will and can be *m*easured. They are *a*ction oriented and *r*ealistic by pointing to attributes that

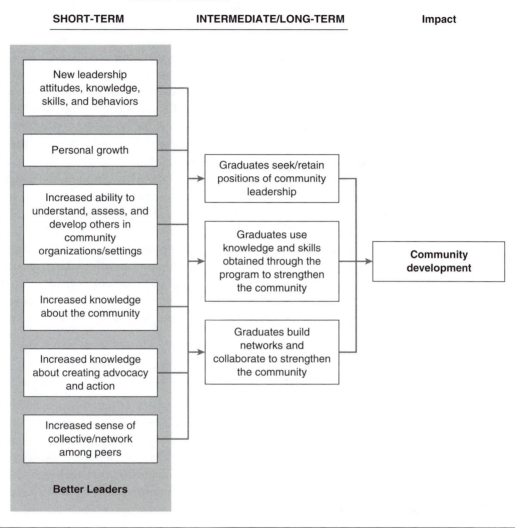

Figure 5.5   Community Leadership Academy Outcome Indicators

demonstrate accomplishments that could occur. They are timed in that they show the order in which they are likely to occur.

In the CLA example (Figure 1.3), the model does not include data collection methods, although evaluation logic models sometimes do. The questions stimulate deeper conversation about evaluation design. In particular, the questions lead to discussion of possible data collection, analysis, and reporting issues. Coverage of evaluation issues beyond the development of basic design questions and indicators is outside the scope of this text.

Data collection methods also influence costs, rigor, and limitations. So, be aware that it is important to take evaluation budget and capacity into account when posing the evaluation questions. In moving from the questions to specifying the methods, it becomes obvious, for most programs, that multiple sources and approaches will be needed to secure information. A short list of the most common data collection methods includes document review, surveys, interviews, focus groups, and observation. Specifying methods in the model helps reinforce the integrated information needs your data collection tools will need to serve. This gives evaluation consumers an opportunity to consider the "burden" they are willing to have their program bear to support the planned evaluation (cost and their time). It also provides insight to the evaluation team on how best to approach data collection in the context of the program and its participants.

The construction of tools (e.g., survey questions, interview protocols) and data analysis can require special expertise. It is important to realize that the placement of questions on the model implies content they will address. In that way, there can be agreement on the outline of what the evaluation will cover and how it will accomplish its purpose. The specific details of measurement and analysis that follow evaluation design are beyond the expertise of most consumers. Thus, the use of logic models to inform these later steps is beyond the scope of this chapter. Readers interested in more detail on evaluation practice (e.g., theory, planning, implementation, and reporting) are referred to the Supplemental Readings list provided at the end of this chapter.

Indicators and Alignment

This model shows what sequence of changes in awareness, knowledge, skills, and behaviors might need to occur to secure the intended impact at some point in the future. It draws on a frequently utilized feature of logic models. Program design and planning with models use a left-to-right, if–then logic; this allows the developers to prospectively examine the pathways whereby their efforts will achieve success. Evaluation, however, can be diagnostic and more retrospective. This is particularly true when evaluation is conducted for the purpose of program improvement. Here, analytic and reflective thinking processes are used to examine and reconstruct the chain of evidence from right to left. It tests the preceding content relative to embedded and named expectations.

There is an additional value to using logic models in evaluation. If you can demonstrate successful achievement of short-term outcomes, you can then use the "logic" described in the model to reasonably assert that your program could make a contribution to outcomes and impact that take longer or that are too fuzzy to evaluate on a tight budget. What was chosen for display and included in the CLA evaluation telegraphs volumes about some of the assumptions underlying the program design and its evaluation. How might the emphases chosen limit the use of evaluation information to improve the program?

Picking appropriate indicators is important. Selecting indicators has meaning relative to the output or outcome each reflects. For example, weight loss could be a process or outcome indicator of improved health—if obesity is a health challenge.

In other circumstances, weight loss may actually be an indicator of health concerns. If student achievement is the outcome sought by a school district, then increased enrollment may not be a good indicator (process or outcome). It could suggest something about the district's financial health, but it may not be the best indicator of student achievement.

The CLA example demonstrates alignment of indicators in that it includes a relatively robust set of process (output) indicators, fairly comprehensive short-term indicators, and a few indicators of outcomes farther out but on the path to community development. Notice that Figure 5.4 (process indicators) and Figure 5.5 (outcome indicators) look different from the logic model shown in Figure 5.3. These two figures illustrate the areas that the evaluation would focus on, not the universe of all possible indicators. This is a display of the information that stakeholders agreed would suffice as evidence of their programs' performance. Typically, in evaluation, another level of detail would show the specific measures that would be used to unpack each indicator. Many times, a table or matrix is used to better manage display because complexity and level of detail can quickly escalate at this stage.

Sometimes indicators are selected and used to communicate progress, but they are not directly or completely, as in the case of the CLA example, connected with intended impact. These "Trojan horses" can be useful for positioning or marketing, but they can confuse authentic evaluation. It is important to make a critical review of the alignment (direct connection, or link) between a selected process or outcome indicator and the path you assert leads to eventual impact.

Results Require Choices

Performance Standards

If expectations (or standards) for performance have been cited, then outputs are an easy place to look for both fidelity (how close to plan) and level (dose) of performance. Sometimes expectations are more detailed and qualified. These are called performance standards. Securing better health may require a particular quantity and quality of exercise. The number of hours and type of exercise can be recorded for any given participant. In mature fields, like education and health, we have considerable knowledge about what works under what conditions. Sometimes our knowledge is precise enough that performance standards have been established. As work is planned and evaluated, standards can be helpful in the pursuit of desired results. The CLA example did not set performance standards initially, but once the evaluation design was complete and data were collected, the group would have the information needed to set expectations for the next round of evaluation.

In the CLA example, new or improved skills among participants are indicators of progress toward outcomes. They are one choice on which to focus inquiry. This deliberate choice about focus can occur because the program is displayed graphically. It is easier to see and choose among areas that have explanatory potential when they are named and displayed in a model (instead of narrative). Evaluation could determine whether or not individuals gained new skills.

At any point of time during the program implementation, inquiry could yield many possibilities. Perhaps, in the case of the CLA evaluation, one discovers no new skills were learned or the skills learned weren't relevant to community development. Maybe skill development for individuals happened but the individuals were never engaged in any community projects. Each of these findings would have implications for program improvement. Alternatively, evaluation could look at curriculum content or even at the list of inputs: participants, faculty, marketing, or other areas. To manage cost and effort in evaluation, choices must be made about where to focus the inquiry.

Quality Evaluation Designs

We believe a quality evaluation design should respond clearly to evaluation consumers and their information needs. In other words, the questions named have utility. As you consider evaluation through the architecture of a logic model, the following questions reflect quality considerations. With colleagues, you might develop additional questions relevant to your workplace, project processes, or content. It is important in evaluation to recall that any model is only one way to represent work. It is a view. During evaluation design it is good to be aware of the many options vying for attention. The same hazards (blind spots, myths, and cultural concerns) that influence circumstances during program design and planning may also present themselves in evaluation. Think about ways to conduct discovery that will identify and resolve these hazards. Multiple models or modeling in service to evaluation provides opportunities to make choices and focus inquiry.

Quality Questions for Evaluation Design

1. Are users of the evaluation specified and ranked relative to priority?

2. Have the information needs of users been specified? What assures use?

3. Will the evaluation improve the work, determine its results, or both?

4. Will the evaluation's key questions meet information needs?

5. Have process indicators been specified and selected for the evaluation?

6. Are there any performance standards established for programs of this type that can assist evaluation?

7. Have outcome indicators been specified and selected for the evaluation?

8. Are the selected outcomes reasonable to expect relative to time and other resources invested in the effort to date?

9. Does the model inform data collection methods?

10. Are stakeholders engaged adequately in the evaluation process (participating when and if appropriate during design, implementation, interpretation) to encourage their use of the findings?

A Quality Framework

Figure 5.6 shows a framework for program and evaluation quality. It assembles the key points from the book's first five chapters. Previously, we described two important standards for model quality: plausibility (theory of change and "could it work") and feasibility (program logic and "will it work under your specific conditions"). The quality characteristics for theory of change models are noted (as in Chapter 2) where the focus is on the relationship between strategies and results.

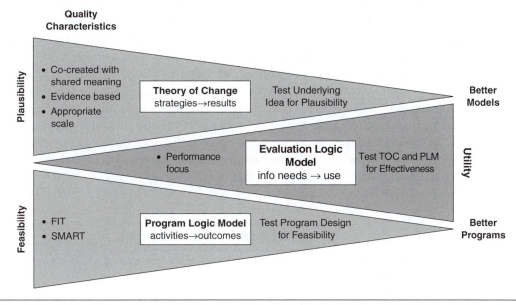

Figure 5.6   Factors and Features of Quality for Program and Evaluation Design

The quality characteristics for program logic models focus on the strength of the relationship between activities and outcomes. The employ FIT (*f*requency, *i*ntensity, and *t*argets) and SMART (*s*pecific, *m*easurable, *a*ction oriented, *r*ealistic, and *t*imed) principles (see Chapter 4). We suggest that logic models for evaluation design be useful. This means they meet the information needs of identified users. It also suggests information gathered is used in the pursuit of performance management and greater effectiveness. We think a program, project, or organization is more likely to achieve impact if relative theory of change models are plausible, program logic models are feasible, and the evaluation models that test the underlying assumptions of each are designed for practical use.

In Summary

In the first half of this book, we posited three questions about effectiveness:

- Are you doing the right work?
- Can you make better decisions?
- Are you getting superior results?

All of these questions, including the third one, require some evaluation literacy. This chapter describes the evaluative thinking and processes logic models can support when effectiveness is given deliberate attention during evaluation. We hope readers will use logic models to contribute to the design of evaluations that will answer these vital questions. They are significantly different from: "Are we busy?" These questions focus attention on effectiveness rather than on efficiency or the accomplishment of a laundry list of activities.

Both formative (improve) and summative (prove) evaluations are useful for many reasons. Both of these approaches can help build understanding about what works under what conditions. Because evaluation is a key function in managing for results, this chapter explains how logic models can assist evaluation design directed toward that end. Models help with decisions about the most relevant information and its use. Identifying and choosing among information needs and users focuses evaluation resources where they are most needed to influence effectiveness. These steps are crucial in creating a useful evaluation. Program evaluation and planning are "bookends" that reflect the same thinking and thus share a common theory of change and very similar program logic model views. Specifically, outputs and outcomes can be very helpful gauges for monitoring and improving the status of your work.

Learning Resources

Reflection

1. What are the strengths and limitations for evaluation when the logic modeling process has already occurred during program development? What about when it occurs after the program is under way?

2. What are the various ways that a theory of change and/or logic model can be used to inform the development of an evaluation design?

3. How might the information needs of funders, grantees, evaluators, and participants be different?

4. What relationships exist among evaluation, logic models, performance management, and effectiveness?

Exercises

1. Based on the program, project, or idea you mapped out in Chapter 4, design the key questions and indicators for its evaluation.

2. Using the health improvement example in Figure 3.4, display your version of key evaluation questions. Cite some process and outcome indicators. Compare your approach to your colleagues'.

3. If the evaluation for the CLA (see Figures 5.4 and 5.5) focuses on two strategies and the impact, what items are completely overlooked and could yield some important information?

References and Supplemental Readings

Texts

Argyris, C. (1993). *Knowledge for action: A guide to overcoming barriers to organizational change.* San Francisco: Jossey-Bass.

Davidson, J. E. (2005). *Evaluation basics: The nuts and bolts of sound evaluation.* Thousand Oaks, CA: Sage.

Fitzpatrick, J. L., Worthen, B. R., & Sanders, J. R. (2004). *Program evaluation: Alternative approaches and practical guidelines* (3rd ed.). Saddle River, NJ: Pearson.

Frechtling, J. (2007). *Logic modeling methods in program evaluation.* San Francisco: Jossey-Bass.

Grantmakers for Effective Organizations. (2007). *Learning for results.* Washington, DC: Author.

Gray, S. T. (Ed.). (1993). *Leadership Independent Sector: A vision of evaluation.* Washington, DC: Independent Sector.

McDavid, J., & Hawthorn, L. (2006). *Program evaluation and performance measurement: An introduction to practice.* Thousand Oaks, CA: Sage.

Patton, M. C. (1996). *Utilization-focused evaluation* (3rd ed.). Thousand Oaks, CA: Sage.

Scriven, M. (1991). *Evaluation thesaurus* (4th ed.). Newbury Park, CA: Sage.

Stufflebeam, D. L. L., & Shinkfield, A. J. (2007). *Evaluation theory, models, and applications.* San Francisco: Jossey-Bass.

The Joint Committee on Standards for Educational Evaluation. (1994). *The program evaluation standards: How to assess evaluations of educational programs* (2nd ed.). Thousand Oaks, CA: Sage.

Woodwell, W. H. (2005). *Evaluation as a pathway to learning.* Washington, DC: Grantmakers for Effective Organizations.

York, P. (2005). *Funder's guide to evaluation: Leveraging evaluation to improve nonprofit effectiveness.* St. Paul, MN: Fieldstone Alliance.

Journal Articles

Adler, M. A. (2002). The utility of modeling in evaluation planning: The case of the coordination of domestic violence services in Maryland. *Evaluation and Program Planning, 25*(3), 203–213.

Carman, J. G. (2007). Evaluation practice among community-based organizations: Research into the reality. *American Journal of Evaluation, 28*(1), 60–75.

Ebrahim, A. (2005). Accountability myopia: Losing sight of organizational learning. *Nonprofit and Voluntary Sector Quarterly, 31,* 56–87.

Forss, K., Cracknell, B., & Samset, K. (1994). Can evaluation help an organization to learn? *Evaluation Review, 18*(5), 574–591.

Howell, E. M., & Yemane (2006). An assessment of evaluation designs: Case studies of 12 large federal evaluations. *American Journal of Evaluation, 27*(2), 219–236.

Kaplan, S. A., & Garrett, K. E. (2005). The use of logic models by community-based initiatives. *Evaluation and Program Planning, 28*(2), 167–172.

Schalock, R. L., & Bonham, G. S. (2003). Measuring outcomes and managing for results. *Evaluation and Program Planning, 26*(3), 229–235.

Trevisan, M. S. (2007). Evaluability assessment from 1986 to 2006. *American Journal of Evaluation, 28*(3), 290–303.

Internet Resources

Innovation Network. (2005). *Evaluation plan workbook.* Washington, DC: Author. Retrieved October 25, 2007, from http://innonet.org/client_docs/File/evaluation_plan_workbook.pdf

Planning and Evaluation Resource Center. (n.d.). Retrieved February 5, 2008, from http://www.evaluationtools.org/

The Urban Institute. (2003). *Developing community-wide outcome indicators for specific services.* Washington, DC: Author. Retrieved February 5, 2008, from http://www.urban.org/UploadedPDF/310813_OutcomeIndicators.pdf

CHAPTER 6

Display and Meaning

This chapter describes selected examples of logic model use. Through brief cases, we present models as used in private and public sector organizations. The variation in format and content are intentional. These models, presented in the context of cases, are provided to enrich readers' experience and experimentation with features of display.

Learner Objectives

- Identify variations in model format and style
- Recognize that models reflect culture and intended use
- Explore what will and will not work in your organization
- Explain why logic models are highly interpretive

Because logic models are socially constructed, perception, politics, and persuasion are all substantial influences on them. As a graphic display of the general approach to change or as a more detailed description of work, logic models reflect intentional choices of their authors. In reality, models can be compromised by the skills and experiences of their creators, along with the context and purposes they serve. Our own models reflect these influences. For example, sometimes clients do not ask for or want modeling ("improved versions"). Although Chapters 2 through 5 in this text have suggested quality features and selected principles for creating models, the examples here vary in adherence. As the use of logic models grows, it is possible that standards for them will emerge and be commonly used. Please note that the cases in this chapter include model examples that have successfully served specific purposes. We identify variation of some key features as important context before sharing the six cases.

Variation and Learning

It is our experience that variation nearly always offers a rich field for learning. In this chapter, the "cases" provide a chance to see actual models and how they look with a range of content and functions. Most of the cases are contributions from colleagues who frequently use logic models. One is an example of our own work with clients. All are influenced by the conditions in which they were created and the people who generated them. And—like most models, all of them could be improved. These examples include both theory of change and program logic models. In several cases, the models are templates or umbrellas for subsequent design/planning and evaluation work. They all serve as "organizers" for a shared understanding and a platform or framework to advance other functions, such as communications, evaluation, planning, and research. Prior to the cases, we describe variations of some key features in models.

Graphic Display

As logic models are tools that show and support critical thinking, the selection of elements used in their display helps illustrate the subject content in a dynamic way. Models avoid some of the interpretation that dense text requires but they are not immune to interpretation. Because logic models convey relationships among elements it is important to be conscious of the use of boxes, lines, curved lines, circles, single- and double-headed arrows, and other shapes in terms of their meaning. Further, their creation occurs in context and has meaning for their creators, and this can vary as they are read by others.

Models in the cases range from pictorial images with copy (Case 4) to circular displays (Case 2) and the most common flowchart style that employs text plus symbols and shapes that are read from left to right. Elements of the models differ, too. Some include inputs, barriers, and facilitators—others do not. Some use arrows, some just lines. Others use neither of these. There is a substantial difference in comprehensiveness. Some are general change recipes while others offer detail adequate to operate a program. In some cases, the models require the case narrative to understand their content. In others, the models are quickly and completely understood without external copy to support them. Cases 1 and 6 show both a theory of change of change and a program logic model.

While the use of graphics to convey meaning can quickly become very sophisticated, most people have had some experience with a model or diagram that contains words and arrows. And all cultures have symbols that convey meaning. Many people, for example, understand that a lightbulb means an idea, crossed swords means conflict, and linked hands means harmony. However, these symbols are cultural and may have no meaning or different meaning in relative context.

Complexity and Meaning

The models shown here and used by practitioners worldwide differ considerably in their complexity. Logic models are often used instead of or as a complement to text because they can simplify and untangle the relationships among elements.

They also can be dense or very simple. Their relative complexity is generally a reflection of the number and type of relationships they are communicating.

For example, the Australian Sustainable Living Program (Case 2) consists of multiple projects that require a framework with shared meaning even though each partner has its own culture. While each partner's day-to-day work is complex and dynamic, their model emphasizes common outcomes in a context of nested influences. In contrast, the model that displays a multi-year, multi-strategy preschool change effort (Case 1) has considerably more detail and a significant number of arrows to communicate influences among features. The preschool model is used for multiple functions: planning, managing, evaluation, and communication. Cases 4 and 1 also demonstrate that models can vary in their relative prescription: from general to very tight and specific. Many times models are used as either an umbrella for a cluster of sub-projects or as a template to guide alignment across a large organization. How tight or loose they are as prescriptions depends on their intended use and the culture of the users.

Moreover, "reading" or interpreting the models in these cases requires entry in different ways. Many are processed left to right, but others are top to bottom or the inverse. Several suggest repeated activity via circular shapes or symbols. And the most pictorial example (Case 4) offers several entry points to the content displayed. There are substantial differences among the models relative to the volume and placement of text.

Content, Uses, and Creation

The subject content for each of the models in our cases is distinct. They include preschool policy change, sustainable living, studentship, collaborative inquiry, diffusion, and the nonprofit sector. Models appear to "work" regardless of the subject matter content. Functionally, they most often serve design/planning, evaluation, and communication. But, we have also seen models that guide research management, organization development, learning, knowledge management, and training.

The model content is informed in various ways. All have multiple stakeholders, and some organizations use theory of change and logic models as standard practice. The development of most of the models was externally supported. Often in real-world situations, the thinking behind a model and its development is not visible to external audiences. Several cases specifically reference theory, evidence, and literature, and they all rely on a continuum of practice experience. While one model required engaging an artist—this is an exception and intentional choice. The sequence of steps and related processes with stakeholders to generate a model varies considerably. This social and technical interaction is very important to the utility and quality of the model produced.

Model Benefits

In all of these cases, the models secure an important process objective: a shared understanding of the work among stakeholders. They all organize and display relationships among multiple features such as strategies, activities, results. And they all provide a common vocabulary and framework for those involved in model creation. Some of the models support operations and others are simply input to the creation of other models or a framework that provides "tent stakes." Regardless of scale (a project, initiative, organization, or other), models can be an important anchor for implementation, evaluation, dissemination, or other next steps because they quickly convey the parameters and content of a bounded effort.

Some models describe an organization's direct and indirect influence, and several of the cases suggest the important implication of time as their models parse outcomes in a sequence or the accompanying narrative references this feature. Time is a particularly important feature to identify in a model and to look for when reading one. Time is not often labeled in years (as in Case 1) but rather in generic qualifiers like "short" and "intermediate." These phrases can have very different meanings among readers. Occasionally, definitive parameters for time are omitted intentionally.

Alternative Approaches

Causal loop diagrams and logical frameworks (also known as logframes) are two other approaches to modeling the connections between "do" and "get." Causal loop diagrams are used to display complex systems behaviors. They highlight the influential forces acting on cause-and-effect relationships. They also show patterns of how and why things change rather than a static snapshot. They have much less text than traditional logic models and are more schematic in appearance. They use interlocking circles, arrows, and other symbols to display cycles. These types of models are most often used by practitioners active in systems thinking and organizational learning.

Logical frameworks grew out of the Management by Objectives movement in the 1970s. They are typically a four by three matrix. The rows describe objectives/goals, purposes, outputs, and activities. The columns address achievement indicators, verification means, and important risks/assumptions. The construction process emphasizes testing the vertical and horizontal logic. These frameworks are widely used internationally by development agencies, nongovernmental agencies, and philanthropies.

In addition to using different elements, logical frameworks differ from logic models in several important ways. Logic models are generative in that they typically emphasize the desired outcomes or impact. In contrast, logical frameworks begin with an analysis of the problem(s) and thus are a more reactive approach. In logic models, the assumptions are propositions upon which the strategies and clusters of activities are based. Alternatively, the assumptions in logical frameworks are those conditions that must exist for the program to be implemented. References for these alternative approaches are provided at the end of this chapter.

Selected Cases

The following cases include both theory of change and program logic models in different formats with different content and uses. We hope that your exposure to these materials helps you to explore important choices as you create models that are most useful to your work and stakeholders. These fascinating examples are shared to display relative diversity. Each and every logic model is distinct—although there are some common features among them. The models and case descriptions were contributed by colleagues in academia, the government, and the private and non-profit sectors. For this reason, there are different emphases and voices for each brief case. At the beginning of each, we suggest one way to read the model and offer comment on selected features. Next, we share the model and associated narrative, contributed by colleagues to offer context for the model. Last, we ask some thought-provoking questions about the display, meaning, and use. Each case also includes some further resources.

All the models in the following cases are versions of an initial effort. When people read (or interpret) a model, they ask: "What is this telling me?" As you explore the cases, it is valuable to consider how the context may have influenced the model. It may also be useful to think how you and your colleagues would create models for the purposes named. What revisions would you make and why? Small changes, just moving a line or element to a different area in the display, can be very significant. We encourage use of the Resources section at this chapter's end because it can help in using these cases for additional learning.

Case 1: Promoting Preschool Change

This case includes three models: a basic theory of change, an expanded theory of change, and a program logic model. The case is about using advocacy to achieve policy change. The basic theory of change model for this case relies on applied political science research. In his well-known research on agenda-setting, political scientist John Kingdon (1995) describes what it takes to get an issue on the public policy agenda. The public policy agenda is the list of issues or problems considered by policymakers. Getting on the agenda. or positioning an item there as a priority involves several processes: problems, proposals, and politics. Kingdon's theory of change model is illustrated in Figure 6.1.

Policy Stream Convergence

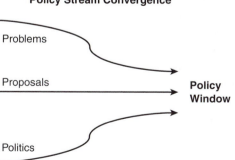

Figure 6.1   Kingdon's Policy Stream Convergence (Coffman, 2007)

In this basic model, the stream of problems, proposals, and politics occurs concurrently for individual policy issues. Problems are the process of persuading policymakers to pay attention. It is "making the case" and defining the reasons a particular issue demands action. Proposals are the process of remedy—their generation, debate, revision, and adoption. And, politics are the many factors that influence the political context. They include climate, culture, and advocacy for and against proposals.

In Kingdon's research, he found the success of agenda-setting was dependent on the three processes. While these three elements operate independently, the actors in each process can overlap or interact. When at least two of the processes intersect at a critical time, then a policy window occurs. These windows represent an opportunity to advance policy on a particular topic or issue.

The expanded theory of change (Figure 6.2) reads from left to right. It shows the connection between the three elements of Kingdon's theory (shaded) with the strategies and outcomes specific to the David and Lucile Packard Foundation's Preschool for California's Children grantmaking program. Packard's Research strategy addresses the policy problem stream. Evidence from research will be used to think about and frame the problems that quality preschool can address. The Leadership and Engagement strategy focuses on the identification and development of policy solutions (proposals) and the building of key leader support for these solutions. The Flagships and Local Strategy serves further to increase visibility and demand. These in turn influence the public and political support for the policy solutions. The three elements of problem, proposals, and politics together open policy windows from which quality preschool policies can emerge. A strong reliance on communication as a support strategy is implied in this model.

The policy stream convergence theory represented by this expanded model is key to reading the program logic model we describe next.

Although ambitious and specific outcomes are named in the Preschool Logic Model (Figure 6.3) at the far right, this model is typically read from left to right. We begin with "inputs" and the column titled Strategies and Activities. The second column details three primary areas of work, which include Leadership and Engagement, Research, Flagships, and Local Strategies.

Leadership and Engagement will cultivate a strong and diverse group of advocates for preschool, both statewide and locally. Research will support projects that reinforce the evidence for preschool value. Flagships and Local Strategies will provide examples of success through support for preschool expansion, quality improvements, and constituency building. Outcomes are parsed by time in three stages: short, intermediate, and long term. This model includes a specific timeline for implementation and outcome achievement. It includes process and outcome indicators shown as bulleted lists within each of the shaded rectangles.

This model ranks strategies and associated outcomes by emphasis. The legend in Figure 6.3 shows that the highest strategic emphasis is shaded the darkest (Intermediate-term Outcomes, Dissemination). The original model also used colored arrows to differentiate and depict relationships connecting strategies/activities with their specific intended outcomes over time. Assumptions about relationships are

Preschool for California's Children Grantmaking Program Strategy

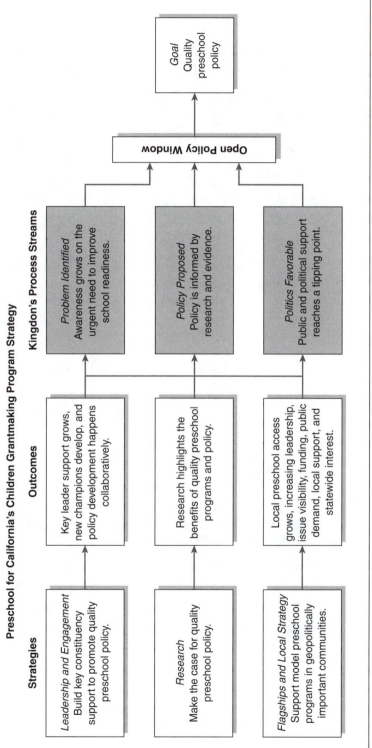

Figure 6.2 Application of Kingdon's Theory to Packard Preschool Program (Coffman, 2007)

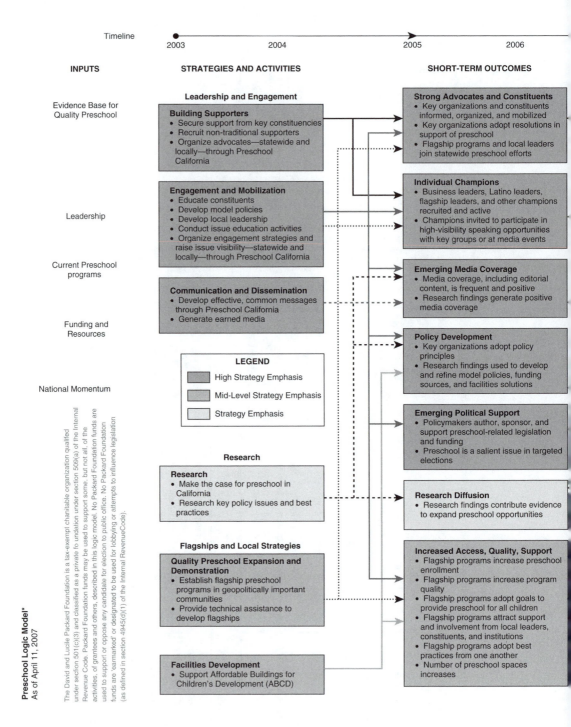

Figure 6.3 Preschool Logic Model (Packard Foundation, 2007)

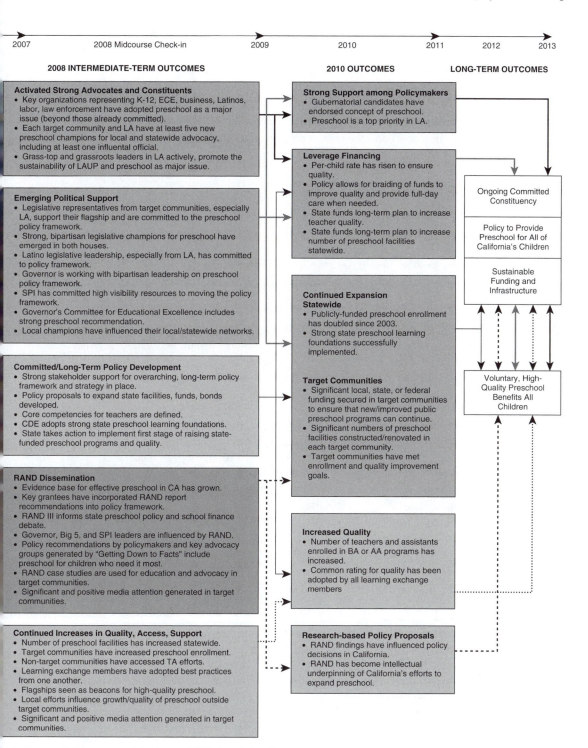

2007   2008 Midcourse Check-in   2009   2010   2011   2012   2013

2008 INTERMEDIATE-TERM OUTCOMES   **2010 OUTCOMES**   **LONG-TERM OUTCOMES**

Activated Strong Advocates and Constituents
- Key organizations representing K-12, ECE, business, Latinos, labor, law enforcement have adopted preschool as a major issue (beyond those already committed).
- Each target community and LA have at least five new preschool champions for local and statewide advocacy, including at least one influential official.
- Grass-top and grassroots leaders in LA actively, promote the sustainability of LAUP and preschool as major issue.

Strong Support among Policymakers
- Gubernatorial candidates have endorsed concept of preschool.
- Preschool is a top priority in LA.

Emerging Political Support
- Legislative representatives from target communities, especially LA, support their flagship and are committed to the preschool policy framework.
- Strong, bipartisan legislative champions for preschool have emerged in both houses.
- Latino legislative leadership, especially from LA, has committed to policy framework.
- Governor is working with bipartisan leadership on preschool policy framework.
- SPI has committed high visibility resources to moving the policy framework.
- Governor's Committee for Educational Excellence includes strong preschool recommendation.
- Local champions have influenced their local/statewide networks.

Leverage Financing
- Per-child rate has risen to ensure quality.
- Policy allows for braiding of funds to improve quality and provide full-day care when needed.
- State funds long-term plan to increase teacher quality.
- State funds long-term plan to increase number of preschool facilities statewide.

Ongoing Committed Constituency

Policy to Provide Preschool for All of California's Children

Sustainable Funding and Infrastructure

Continued Expansion Statewide
- Publicly-funded preschool enrollment has doubled since 2003.
- Strong state preschool learning foundations successfully implemented.

Committed/Long-Term Policy Development
- Strong stakeholder support for overarching, long-term policy framework and strategy in place.
- Policy proposals to expand state facilities, funds, bonds developed.
- Core competencies for teachers are defined.
- CDE adopts strong state preschool learning foundations.
- State takes action to implement first stage of raising state-funded preschool programs and quality.

Target Communities
- Significant local, state, or federal funding secured in target communities to ensure that new/improved public preschool programs can continue.
- Significant numbers of preschool facilities constructed/renovated in each target community.
- Target communities have met enrollment and quality improvement goals.

Voluntary, High-Quality Preschool Benefits All Children

RAND Dissemination
- Evidence base for effective preschool in CA has grown.
- Key grantees have incorporated RAND report recommendations into policy framework.
- RAND III informs state preschool policy and school finance debate.
- Governor, Big 5, and SPI leaders are influenced by RAND.
- Policy recommendations by policymakers and key advocacy groups generated by "Getting Down to Facts" include preschool for children who need it most.
- RAND case studies are used for education and advocacy in target communities.
- Significant and positive media attention generated in target communities.

Increased Quality
- Number of teachers and assistants enrolled in BA or AA programs has increased.
- Common rating for quality has been adopted by all learning exchange members

Continued Increases in Quality, Access, Support
- Number of preschool facilities has increased statewide.
- Target communities have increased preschool enrollment.
- Non-target communities have accessed TA efforts.
- Learning exchange members have adopted best practices from one another.
- Flagships seen as beacons for high-quality preschool.
- Local efforts influence growth/quality of preschool outside target communities.
- Significant and positive media attention generated in target communities.

Research-based Policy Proposals
- RAND findings have influenced policy decisions in California.
- RAND has become intellectual underpinning of California's efforts to expand preschool.

implied by the arrows among elements. This quantity of arrows depicts a highly interactive and integrated body of work. Arrowheads show that the majority of the relationships are one way, indicating progress toward outcomes moving toward the right. Four named outcomes indicate intentions for comprehensive and specific change in the right-most column. Double-headed arrows here (Long-Term Outcomes) illustrate the reciprocal and likely amplifying relationship between the connected cluster of terminal outcomes and the overarching result of quality preschool.

The Preschool for California's Children logic model is a graphic representation of the David and Lucile Packard Foundation's preschool grantmaking program. Within the Packard Foundation, Preschool for California's Children is referred to as a subprogram, and it is within the broader Children, Families and Communities Program. It depicts our core grantmaking strategies and illustrates how we expect funded activities to produce outputs and outcomes that build toward the ultimate goal of voluntary, high-quality preschool for all of California's 3- and 4-year-olds.

The original logic model was created by program staff, but was later modified in collaboration with the external evaluation design process. The logic model flows from a theory of change advanced by political scientist John Kingdon, who posited that policy change occurs when three catalytic elements (problem, policy, politics) come together at the same time. Advocates must seize upon the window of opportunities when these three streams converge.

This program logic model translates the theory of change into a detailed plan of action, connecting activities to outputs to short-, intermediate-, and long-term outcomes over time. It contains three core strategies: Leadership and Engagement, Research, and Flagships and Local Strategies. It is expected that the combination of outcomes from all three strategies will generate increasing progress toward outcomes. It is important to note that the three core strategies are all interconnected. For example, in this logic model, if one follows the flagship strategy of Quality Preschool Expansion and Demonstration horizontally across the page, one observes a number of significant local outcomes related to access and quality. However, more pivotal to achieving the big win, flagships will also contribute "vertically" to leadership and engagement goals of recruiting champions, generating media coverage, growing public support, and providing models for policy development.

The Preschool Logic Model is a useful graphic for understanding the effort, but it is also an important planning tool for evaluation. Evaluators use logic models to provide a blueprint for evaluation, interpret evaluation results, and facilitate contingency planning. Based on the preschool logic model, the Harvard Family Research Project evaluation team identified evaluation questions, outcomes to be examined, and indicators to measure those outcomes. The logic model also provides insight into timing, for setting prospective benchmarks, scheduling data collection, and subsequently gauging whether sufficient progress has been made. Where progress isn't happening, the anticipated connections between the boxes in the logic model may not form, inducing us to make midcourse corrections or rethink parts of our strategy and modify the logic model. The program logic model is malleable; activities and their associated indicators may change in response to contingencies, but the fundamental theory remains constant. This model is a revised version.

At the Packard Foundation, both theory of change and logic model are essential components of good programmatic strategy development and management necessary to help us achieve greater impact in our work. Theory of change and logic models are developed, reviewed, and/or revised for many reasons.

For us, a theory of change serves as a tool with three purposes: planning, communication, and monitoring. First, developing a theory of change encourages strategic thinking, as one clarifies the connections between desired outcomes and the strategies and activities designed to achieve them. It illuminates underlying assumptions, explores the larger system in which the change will take place, and brings to bear relevant evidence or experience in support of the assumptions.

Second, by making specific the desired outcomes, strategic pathways, and underlying assumptions, a theory of change promotes transparency and provides a platform for engagement with stakeholders, particularly grantees. Grantee partners should be able to understand the theory of change and connect their work to it. A theory of change helps to clarify roles and expectations.

Finally, the theory of change serves as a basis for the monitoring and evaluating approach. Since the theory of change helps to describe the assumptions that their work is testing, it points to what needs to be assessed in a monitoring plan.

We believe that theory of change and logic models should be developed by engaging multiple perspectives and drawing on existing knowledge and experience. Grantees, stakeholders, experts, and Foundation staff can and should be engaged. In defining the landscape, outside experts can be very helpful in developing background papers or other inputs that can inform the development of the framework. Given their central role in implementing the theory of change, grantees must be engaged at some stage. The subprogram staff lead is the primary architect of the theory of change and logic model.

Questions

1. What features do you like and dislike in this model? Why?

2. What are other ways you can imagine the content of this model displayed?

3. Would a model like this one get use in your workplace?

4. Is the comprehensiveness of this model helpful or overwhelming? Why?

5. What key evaluation questions are inferred by the model?

6. Could you prepare a request for proposal from this model that would assist grantmaking? Why or why not?

References

For more about the David and Lucile Packard Foundation, see: http://www .packard.org

Coffman, J. (2007). Evaluations to watch: Evaluation based on theories of the policy process. *Evaluation Exchange, 13*(1). Retrieved February 11, 2008, from http://www.gse .harvard.edu/hfrp/eval/issue34/eval2.html

Kingdon, J. W. (1995). *Agendas, alternatives and public policies* (2nd ed.). New York: Longman.

Case 2: Australian Sustainable Living Program

The Our Earth—It's a Living Thing (OEILT) Model (Figure 6.4) has three primary elements. In the center is a hierarchy of intended meta-outcomes that reflect multiple projects in the partnership. Most readers might begin at this listing. These outcomes are influenced by the darker, internal ring of features, including partnership effectiveness, program management, project activities, and outputs. The external ring represents the context, specifically the features outside the individual projects and overall program that in turn influence progress toward desired outcomes.

While some elements of the rings are not detailed, the outcomes are precise and shown to occur in a specific order. Outcomes occur in sequence from rectangle 1 through 7, moving from bottom to top of the outcome chain. For example, rectangle 1 shows that participation and exposure to program messages must precede any increase in awareness among participants in rectangle 2 and so on up the line. However, the arrow going directly from rectangle 2 to rectangle 6 also shows that, in some cases, some of the intermediate steps may be bypassed. Increased awareness and concern may be sufficient to generate action without the program needing to do anything to increase knowledge and skills. People may already know what to do but lack the concern to do it. For most members of the target audiences, however, the model for the educational program has been constructed around the need to generate awareness before it can go on to generate interest and in turn implement activities that will increase knowledge, skills, and new actions. The model was drawn to show that not everyone would have to go in a lockstep manner through every level of outcome. The path as depicted would depend on the factors in the outer ring. Also that the achievement of one level of outcome does not automatically lead to the next level but that the program needs to take action to move its audience up the ladder.

Also of note, this model makes it clear that desired outcomes will occur only among those who hear the "message" and that the effort depends on those it targets to in turn influence others. Arrows in the model convey interaction among levels and between outcomes. This model clearly communicates the "nested" nature of the program by presenting text in a ladder and surrounding it with other layers. It also shows a feedback loop between the terminal outcome 7 back to the beginning. We would interpret this to mean that as programs are successful, communication of these results can be used to create and spread new rounds of messages about sustainable living.

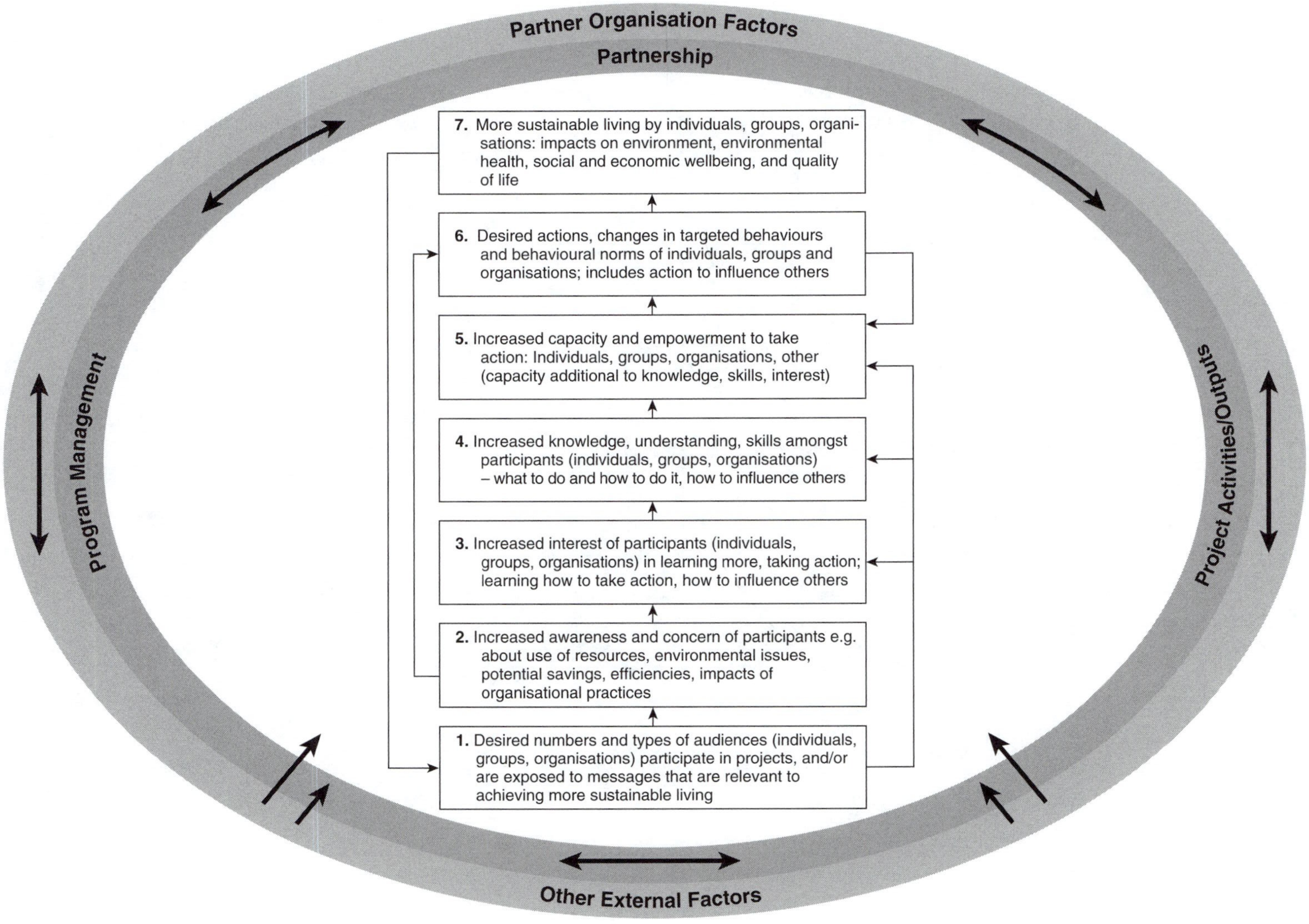

Partner Organisation Factors
Partnership
7. More sustainable living by individuals, groups, organisations: impacts on environment, environmental health, social and economic wellbeing, and quality of life
6. Desired actions, changes in targeted behaviours and behavioural norms of individuals, groups and organisations; includes action to influence others
5. Increased capacity and empowerment to take action: Individuals, groups, organisations, other (capacity additional to knowledge, skills, interest)
4. Increased knowledge, understanding, skills amongst participants (individuals, groups, organisations) – what to do and how to do it, how to influence others
3. Increased interest of participants (individuals, groups, organisations) in learning more, taking action; learning how to take action, how to influence others
2. Increased awareness and concern of participants e.g. about use of resources, environmental issues, potential savings, efficiencies, impacts of organisational practices
1. Desired numbers and types of audiences (individuals, groups, organisations) participate in projects, and/or are exposed to messages that are relevant to achieving more sustainable living
Program Management
Project Activities/Outputs
Other External Factors

Figure 6.4 Our Environment—It's a Living Thing (OEILT) Model (Funnell, 2006)

There are underlying communication and individual behavior change theories implied by this model. An education program, primarily reflecting social learning theory, was adopted because a lack of awareness, knowledge, and skills had been identified as key barriers to change for the audiences with which the program worked. Other audiences may be affected more by the use of other policy tools, such as incentives and sanctions (carrots and sticks).

The model discussed in this example relates to a 2-year program that focused on influencing the "sustainable living" behavior of people at home, at work, and at play through a range of community education elements. The program, funded by a state government, was managed and implemented by a partnership that consists of state government departments, an association for local community service organizations, several large nonprofit environmental organizations, and a social welfare organization. Eleven projects are being operated through the program via a partnership. Some are run solely or primarily by one or another of the partner organizations, and some projects are run by several or all organizations collaboratively. They are united by a common commitment to improving sustainable living but differ with respect to target audiences, specific objectives, and ways of operating.

Among the partners, there was no shared theory of change underpinning the program. Given the very different types of organizations involved it would be reasonable to assume that they would bring different values and philosophies to the program. An evaluation framework was commissioned that was to be sensitive to and sufficiently flexible to incorporate these different perspectives. The evaluation would provide a useful basis for designing, implementing, and reporting the ongoing formative evaluation and summative evaluation. The evaluator developed and applied the framework, taking into consideration specific challenges for evaluating partnership programs (Funnell, 2006). The evaluator was also to play an evaluation capacity building role in relation to the partners. This included development of their capacity with respect to the use of logic models.

The OEILT logic model was created using multiple sources of information and in collaboration with the partners. It had multiple uses, including communicate program rationale, support evaluation design, foster common purposes, and assist with project development and management. Importantly, it was also used to assist each of the 11 projects to generate a more detailed logic that was specific to it. These project specific logics were consistent with the approach described in Funnell (2000), including outcomes, attributes of success, outputs, activities, and indicators. These project-specific models were nested in the overall logic model illustrated here. Both the overall and project-specific logics were then used to work with projects to identify the data that would be collected for the evaluation and to report the findings for projects and the program as a whole.

Staff in this project were receptive to the logic model process. In particular, the lead agency (Department of Environment and Conservation) was a keen advocate of the use of logic models. The primary value of the model was conceptual coherence, the development of a common sense of purpose and an evaluation/reporting framework for a group of otherwise loosely related projects brought together as a partnership and encouraged to work together as a genuine program, sharing target audiences, sharing education strategies, developing common messages, and so on. The pictorial nature and simplicity of the model assisted with its acceptance even though in some respects its simplicity also stimulated much debate. Its adaptability to individual projects, use of common concepts, and combining of a relatively small number of common indicators with project-specific indicators proved to be important features contributing to its success.

Fostering a partnership was a goal of the funding agency. The logic model showed that the effective operation of the partnership would be a key factor influencing the success of the program. Accordingly, both the formative and summative evaluations incorporated measurement of the health and dynamics of the partnership. Several tools were used to monitor and evaluate the partnership (Hardy, Hudson, & Waddington, 2003). Feedback was provided to partners to improve the functioning of the partnership and to identify lessons that would be relevant for future partnerships.

Questions

1. Which features in this model communicate most clearly? Why?

2. Why are the external rings important to the OEILT model?

3. As you read the model, do the types of arrows signal specific relationships?

4. What is most clear in this graphic? Why? What is confusing? Why?

5. What are other ways to display the content shown here?

References

Bemelsmans-Videc, M., Rist, R., & Vedung, E. (1998). *Carrots, sticks and sermons: Policy instruments and their evaluation.* Edison, NJ: Transaction Publishers.

Department of Environment and Conservation, NSW. (2005). *Does your project make a difference?* Retrieved October 25, 2007, from http://www.environment.nsw.gov.au/community/projecteval.htm

Funnell, S. (2000). Developing and using a program theory matrix for program evaluation and performance monitoring. *New Directions for Evaluation, 87,* 91–101.

Funnell, S. (2006, September). *Evaluating partnership programs: Challenges and approaches.* Paper presented at the 2006 Annual Conference of the Australasian Evaluation Society. Retrieved October 25, 2007, from http://www.aes.asn.au/conferences/

Hardy, B., Hudson, B., & Waddington, E. (2003). *Assessing strategic partnership: The partnership assessment tool.* London: Office of the Deputy Prime Minister.

Case 3: Canadian Studentship Program

The MD/PhD Studentship Award Program Logic Model (Figure 6.5) has two gross parts: processes and outcomes. Starting at the far left column, features are read from top to bottom (1–3). This far left column shows the work of the Alberta Heritage Foundation for Medical Research. These inputs support implementation and generate outputs, completing the process side with an operating MD/PhD program at two universities. The outcome side of the model is read left to right (4–6). The University of Alberta and the University of Calgary (UA/C) MD/PhD Programs each contribute to short-, intermediate-, and long-term outcomes. This model draws on Dressler's (1980) organization theory to connect program structures with desired behavior change among participants in ways that benefit the medical field and the province.

The model in Figure 6.5 uses numbers to order sequence and it specifies when intermediate- and long-term outcomes are anticipated to occur. It also employs two kinds of arrows to show relationships among features as processes contribute to outcomes over time. The larger shaded arrows are used to show the collective influence of process components (foundation and university partners) on the left moving toward desired outcomes across increasing breadth (participants, medical field, province) on the right. Smaller arrows are used to show the progression over time from clusters of short-term to intermediate- and long-term outcomes. Groups of outcomes are clustered as bulleted lists within each set to provide detail. The display relies on clear "if–then" logic that predicts if the processes occur, then the outcomes will result as a consequence.

The MD/PhD Studentship Award Program Logic Model was developed to evaluate the Alberta Heritage Foundation for Medical Research (AHFMR) MD/PhD Studentship Award Program and determine its continuance. The MD/PhD training programs are offered at two universities in the Province of Alberta, Canada. Their goal is to reduce the disparity between research and application of the findings in medical and health-related fields by training exceptional students to become clinician–scientists through simultaneous completion of MD and PhD degrees. In 1997, AHFMR began to provide financial support for MD/PhD students at the two universities. This consisted of a 2-year stipend and a small research allowance, renewable for up to 6 years with the condition that the universities "topped up" the amount awarded to each student by 15%.

In 2005, the MD/PhD Evaluation Advisory Group was formed to oversee a formative evaluation of the program. It was composed of representatives from the three key stakeholders; namely, AHFMR and the two universities' Faculties of Medicine. The Advisory Group developed an evaluation project outline that detailed the purpose, a list of 15 key evaluation questions, and a timeline for the evaluation process. Two "big" questions were of interest: the merit and significance of the program and how could it be improved through evaluation findings.

A representative Advisory Group was involved in developing this model. The program outcomes were named and resulted in new awareness of feasible expectations. This understanding modified expectations for the evaluation. The results of the evaluation confirmed the program's value and helped stakeholders to understand when a process-oriented evaluation would be useful. The evaluation also raised a number of programmatic issues that were discussed by the Advisory Group.

This two-pronged process model addresses the loose linkages often found between the funder and the programs under study. This model has particular resonance with clients who have limited control over program outcomes and who feel removed from the interactions associated with program activities. In the past, either the funder's processes or funded programs' processes were subsumed in a broader, single-strand logic model that did not reflect either of their realities. This new conceptualization seems to address some of their concerns.

At Barrington Research Group, Inc., we typically prepare a program theory in collaboration with our clients for each evaluation study we conduct prior to designing either a data collection plan or the evaluation tools. In this way, the program "universe" is defined before moving forward into tool design and data collection, analysis, synthesis, and interpretation. While time consuming, the shared understanding that results provides appropriate parameters for stakeholders' expectations of evaluation processes and findings.

Questions

1. What graphic features are most helpful to you in reading the model? What is confusing? Why?

2. Why might it be important to distinguish the work of the foundation from the work at the university sites?

3. What evaluation questions are suggested by this model? Are there questions you would add that the model does not suggest?

4. How could you display this program content differently?

References

For further information, see: http://www.barringtonresearchgrp.com.

Alberta Heritage Foundation for Medical Research. (2007). *Mission statement.* Retrieved August 20, 2007, from http://www.ahfmr.ab.ca/about.php

Dessler, G. (1980). *Organization theory: Integrating structure and behavior.* Englewood Cliffs, NJ: Prentice Hall.

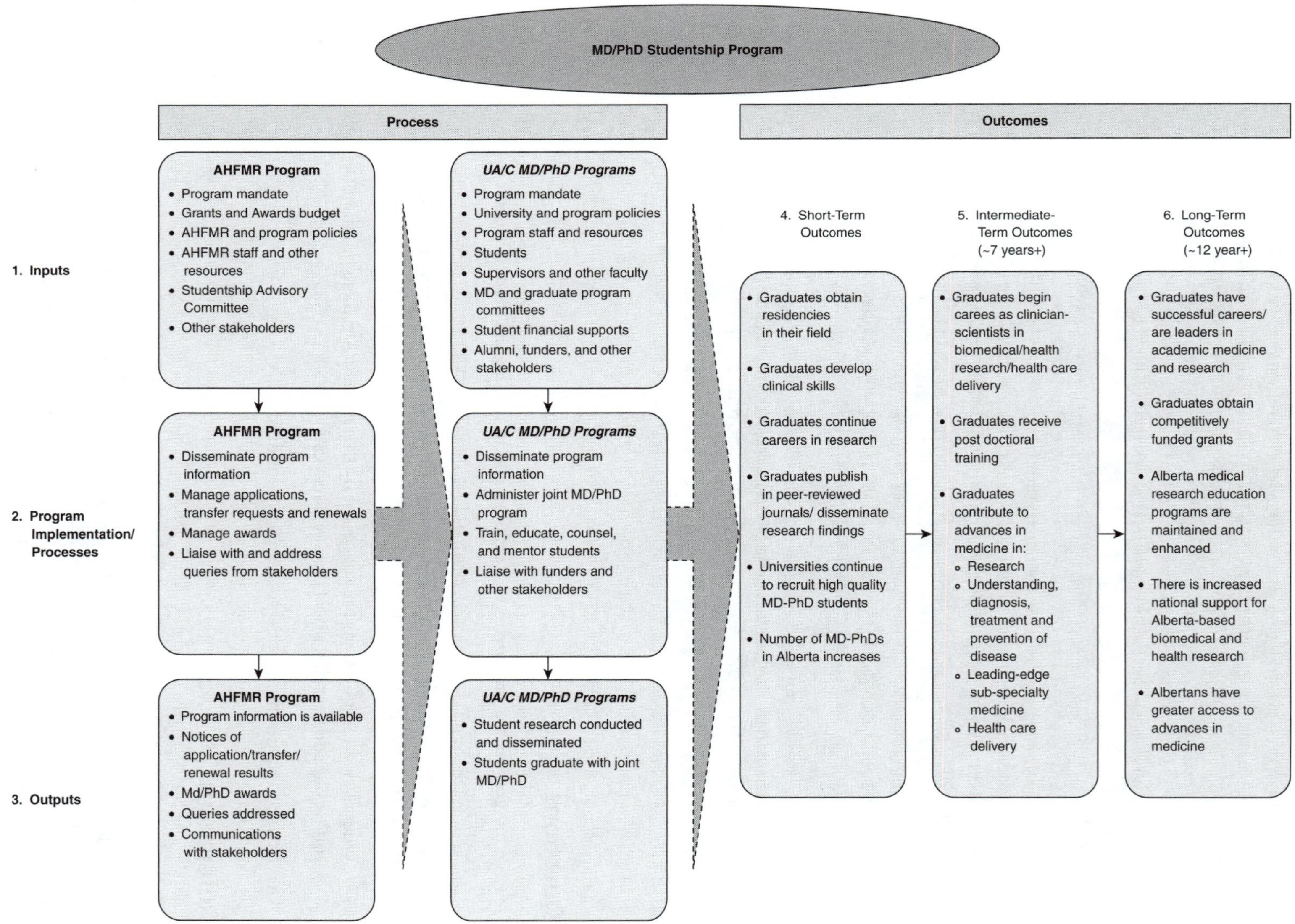

Figure 6.5 MD/PhD Studentship Program (Barrington et al., 2007)

MD/PhD Studentship Program

Process

Outcomes

1. Inputs

AHFMR Program
- Program mandate
- Grants and Awards budget
- AHFMR and program policies
- AHFMR staff and other resources
- Studentship Advisory Committee
- Other stakeholders

UA/C MD/PhD Programs
- Program mandate
- University and program policies
- Program staff and resources
- Students
- Supervisors and other faculty
- MD and graduate program committees
- Student financial supports
- Alumni, funders, and other stakeholders

2. Program Implementation/ Processes

AHFMR Program
- Disseminate program information
- Manage applications, transfer requests and renewals
- Manage awards
- Liaise with and address queries from stakeholders

UA/C MD/PhD Programs
- Disseminate program information
- Administer joint MD/PhD program
- Train, educate, counsel, and mentor students
- Liaise with funders and other stakeholders

3. Outputs

AHFMR Program
- Program information is available
- Notices of application/transfer/ renewal results
- Md/PhD awards
- Queries addressed
- Communications with stakeholders

UA/C MD/PhD Programs
- Student research conducted and disseminated
- Students graduate with joint MD/PhD

4. Short-Term Outcomes
- Graduates obtain residencies in their field
- Graduates develop clinical skills
- Graduates continue careers in research
- Graduates publish in peer-reviewed journals/ disseminate research findings
- Universities continue to recruit high quality MD-PhD students
- Number of MD-PhDs in Alberta increases

5. Intermediate- Term Outcomes (~7 years+)
- Graduates begin careers as clinician- scientists in biomedical/health research/health care delivery
- Graduates receive post doctoral training
- Graduates contribute to advances in medicine in:
  ◦ Research
  ◦ Understanding, diagnosis, treatment and prevention of disease
  ◦ Leading-edge sub-specialty medicine
  ◦ Health care delivery

6. Long-Term Outcomes (~12 year+)
- Graduates have successful careers/ are leaders in academic medicine and research
- Graduates obtain competitively funded grants
- Alberta medical research education programs are maintained and enhanced
- There is increased national support for Alberta-based biomedical and health research
- Albertans have greater access to advances in medicine

Case 4: Collaborative Learning, Inquiry, and Practice

Reading this distinct illustration-type logic model (Figure 6.6) could start at several different points of entry along a path or road-like arrow from left to right. The relative size and strength of the word *impact* draws attention to the far right side of the display. Intellectually, the impacts listed for participants/members encourage the reader to search out information about the "CLIPs" to understand how this term is defined. Information that typically on a logic model might be labeled as inputs, activities, and resources is placed as precursors on the path that weaves across the diagram. Moving to the far left corner, it feels natural to explore the "key features," "relationship emphasis," and "the three inquiry steps" that provide information about the program much like the activities column in a more traditional model. Notice the spiral encircling the person; this likely infers the iterative nature of the inquiry process. Dropping down the model to the lower left corner, the "supporting structures" are defined, and these are similar to the type of information in an input column. The relationship "guiding principles" follow, and these describe attributes of CLIPs that could be interpreted as shorter-term outcomes for the CLIP process that contribute to member impact.

This model also uses a vine to organize features in relationship to each other. Male and female figures are strategically placed with positive, energetic postures. Signs and pages with text are repeating features that are used to draw the reader's attention from left to right instead of boxes and arrows. Several sizes and styles of font are also used in what could be interpreted as a hierarchy of importance. This program draws on a broad literature base, grounded in evaluative and appreciative inquiry, to validate the strength and direction of relationships among inputs, activities, outcomes, and impact as displayed.

Communities of Learning, Inquiry, and Practice (CLIPs) are self-selected informal, dynamic groups of community college faculty and/or staff (and sometimes others) who conduct an inquiry about a topic they identify and see as important. The inquiry steps are (1) design the inquiry, (2) collect data, and (3) make meaning and shape practice. Through participation in the CLIP, members build their capacity to collaboratively conduct such inquiries and enhance their professional practice. A member within each CLIP serves as its Facilitator. An overall CLIP Guide positions the CLIPs at the college and supports the CLIP work by handling coordination, organization, and financial matters related to CLIP work.

CLIPs provide opportunities for community college faculty and staff to collaboratively study issues of importance to them about student learning and success. CLIPs add vitality to institutionally determined assessment, program review, and planning processes. The CLIP process is being developed through an evaluative research study at Bakersfield College conducted by InSites (a nonprofit organization) under a National Science Foundation grant (Grant Number REC-0335581). The purpose of the grant is to develop the CLIP process as an evaluation capacity building process.

To construct the theory of change/logic model for the CLIP process, I drew on the data I gathered as part of the research in my role as the first CLIP Guide. I also used data gathered by our external formative evaluators. Using these data, I worked with a visual artist to create the model.

The diagram is used to help people who are involved in CLIPs keep the big picture in mind concerning their work. It also is used to inform others of the CLIP process (through conferences, meetings, and online) and to recruit additional CLIPs. It has been made into a poster 3' × 4' so it can be displayed on walls in meetings. We have given people 8.5 × 11-inch copies to reference to keep the whole process in mind and where they are in that process. The diagram depicts individual CLIPs within a college. This version is the second version of the model. Initially, Guiding Principles were not included because they had not yet been determined.

One challenge in developing this type of diagram is finding a visual artist to work with you to create it. Another challenge is keeping it updated since it is expensive to have an artist redo it. It raises the question of how long you can use a diagram when it doesn't quite represent the project anymore. We found that it was still very useful and we could describe the changes that were emerging as the research continued. The diagram was a fine tool for working with the people who were directly involved in the project and having them seeing their experiences captured visually. It helped them put all the pieces together and to share their experience with others. In this case, I think "a picture is worth a thousand words" was very true. The shortest description we had when we first developed the diagram was four pages. This visual with the human figures gave the four pages life, personalization, and meaning. Its colorfulness also attracted people's attention.

Questions

1. Would this style of model have appeal in your organization? Why or why not?

2. What skills and resources would be important in creating models in this format?

3. What significance do the vine, signs, pages, and figures have for you? Would others share your interpretation?

4. In what other ways could you display the content of this model?

5. How does this model compare and contrast to others in this chapter?

References

Online modules are available for people to learn how to implement CLIPs on their campus. The modules are available free through the InSites Web site at www.insites.org. The modules can be downloaded and adapted to other contexts.

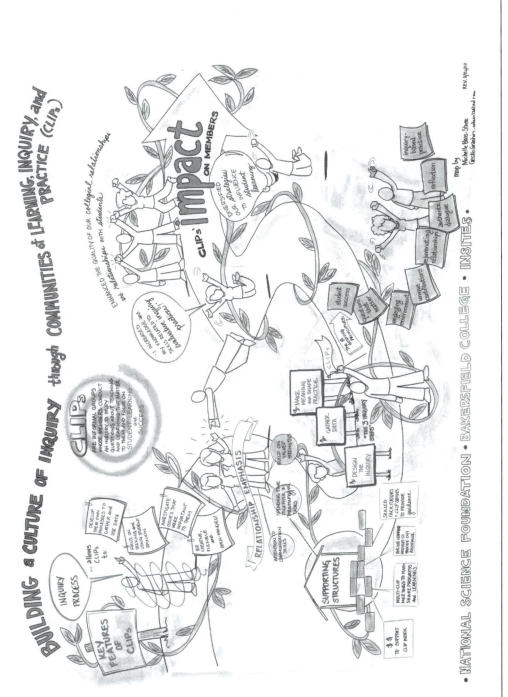

Figure 6.6 Communities of Learning, Inquiry, and Practice Model (Parsons, 2006)

Brown, J., & Isaacs, D. (2005). *The world café: Shaping our futures through conversations that matter.* San Francisco: Berrett-Koehler.

Hughes, P. M. (2004). *Gracious space: A practical guide for working better together.* Seattle: Center for Ethical Leadership.

Maki, P. (2004). *Assessing for learning: Building a sustainable commitment across the institution.* Sterling, VA: Stylus.

Mohr, B., & Watkins, J. (2002). *The essentials of appreciative inquiry: A roadmap for creating positive futures.* Waltham, MA: Pegasus Communications.

Parsons, B. (2002). *Evaluative inquiry: Using evaluation to promote student success.* Thousand Oaks, CA: Corwin Press.

Case 5: Diffusing Ideas and Technologies

This model (Figure 6.7) is read most easily read from top to bottom. It begins with the top layer of the model, showing that the U.S. Department of Energy's Energy Efficiency and Renewable Energy (EERE) programs serve specific functions (e.g., build infrastructure, fund and promote adoption). The detail of the first layer reads from left to right and outlines a sequential set of activities, ignoring feedback loops. The next layer in the model specifies target audiences and partners with and for whom the corresponding outputs are produced. Rogers's diffusion of innovations theory was used as a basis for this generic model, which can then be used to tailor specific strategies for each of the audiences named. What is not a program strategy is taken into consideration as external mediating factors. Then, expected behavior of the targets and partners are described. These are likely short- and intermediate-term outcomes. Multiple long-term program outcomes that follow from these intermediate outcomes appear in boxed text at the bottom of the model. This model is part of a set of nested logic models, including detailed logics for each of the target audience domains.

Several shapes and arrow styles are used in this model. It relies on text that reads in a logical sequence that is very similar to narrative. This model presents a visual paragraph as an alternative to the traditional flowchart type model. Moving from top to bottom (in order) is a distinct feature. Ovals are used to highlight the "do" portion at the top and the "get" portion at the bottom.

The U.S. Department of Energy (DOE) Office of Energy Efficiency and Renewable Energy (EERE) is an organization with multiple offices and programs that primarily conducts energy research but also promotes technology delivery through products and services designed to induce the adoption of energy efficient technologies and practices. EERE addresses wind, solar, hydrogen, and biomass technologies; the efficient use of energy in residential, commercial, and industrial structures and operations; reduced energy use in government buildings and low-income residences; appliance standards; and more. At the request of the EERE's Office of Planning, Budget and Analysis, we developed a series of related generic logic models for deployment programs to describe the multiple causal paths for the diffusion of a new idea, technology or practice.

The DOE logic model is a generic description of how EERE deployment programs produce impacts. At the topmost level, EERE deployment programs analyze and plan; build infrastructure; fund and promote the adoption of new technologies; and review, evaluate, and report. EERE targets and partners with knowledge workers, government officials, market players, and end users, depending on where DOE deems help can be most useful, where DOE has capabilities, and where there is a good fit with DOE's mission.

To varying degrees, EERE deployment programs undertake activities to influence audiences in four areas: knowledge, public policy and public organizations and institutions, market, and end user. The areas operate as a system. In general, deployment programs have neither the staff nor the resources to continuously stimulate actions in these areas or to touch all possible actors. It is through replication, emulation, and the internalization of the meaning of the actions that efficient technologies and practices will be incorporated more broadly within the culture.

Evaluators from diverse academic fields (sociology and economics) who are familiar with evaluation, social science theories, and the U.S. DOE programs, were primarily responsible for developing the generic diffusion logic models. We had previously developed numerous logic models for EERE and other technology deployment programs, working with program managers and staff. EERE has utilized logic models in parts of the organization for more than 10 years. This utilization is increasing, and some of the increased use can be attributed to provision of generic, theory-based logic models. This set of logic models and the evaluation framework built around them included input from managers of EERE deployment programs and a more formal review by an external expert panel of evaluators and potential users of the models and the evaluation framework.

Rather than ask users to create a theory of change, we have adapted Everett Rogers's diffusion theory of social change to the outcome space, providing a generic model for each area. This makes it easier for program managers and evaluators to understand the effects their programs are having, develop more realistic logic models, and therefore to design and conduct better evaluations. For the larger portfolio of EERE programs, the generic templates based on a common theoretical model offer an approach to developing more consistent metrics and measures across programs allowing better defense of the program and greater opportunity to aggregate these effects.

Questions

1. How do the shading, ellipses, rectangles, text, and arrows lead the reader through the model?

2. Would this style of model work in your organization? Why or why not?

3. How would you draw this content and the relationship among elements?

4. Do you think the generic nature of this model and its use influence its features? Why or why not?

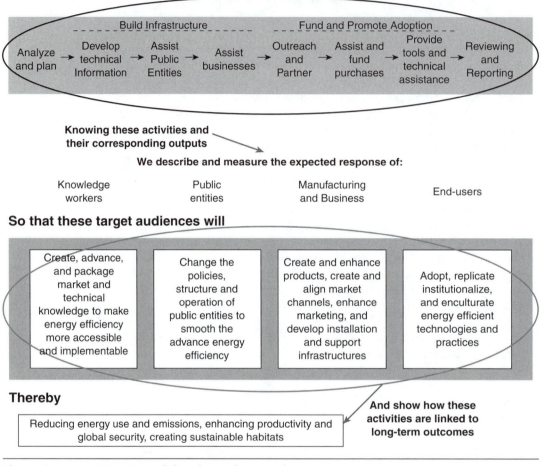

Figure 6.7   DOE Framework (Reed & Jordan, 2007)

References

Reed, J. H. (2006). *A generic, theory-based logic model for creating scientifically based program logic models.* Paper presented at the American Evaluation Association, Portland, OR. Retrieved October 25, 2007, from http://www.wren-network.net/resources/2006AEA/11-%20Creating%20Scientifically-based%20RTD%20Logic%20Models/Reed%20Jordan%20AEA20062.ppt

Reed, J. H., & Jordan, G. B. (2007). Using systems theory and logic models to define integrated outcomes and performance measures in multi-program settings. *Research Evaluation, 16*(3), 169–181.

Reed, J. H., Jordan, G. B., & Vine, E. (2007). Impact evaluation framework for technology deployment programs: An approach for quantifying retrospective energy savings, clean energy advances and market effects. Washington, DC: U.S. Department of Energy. Retrieved October 25, 2007, from http://www.evalframework.org

Rogers, E. (2003). *Diffusion of innovations.* New York: Free Press.

Vine, E., Jordan, G. B., Reed, J. H., & Dowd, J. (2006). An inside look at a U.S. Department of Energy impact evaluation framework for deployment programs. *Proceedings of the 2006 ACEEE Summer Study on Energy Efficiency in Building, 12,* 103–114. Washington, DC: ACEEE.

Case 6: Evaluation System Development

This example includes both a theory of change and a program logic model. The Independent Sector (IS) theory of change model is read from left to right (Figure 6.8). IS work begins with their efforts, as an organization, to strengthen, lead, and mobilize their members, who influence the sector and ultimately generate two primary outcomes.

This model employs arrows and text only. It is simple and displays an explanation of how change is expected to happen. IS influence is characterized in two ways: direct and indirect. The most direct influence is that which IS has on its members;

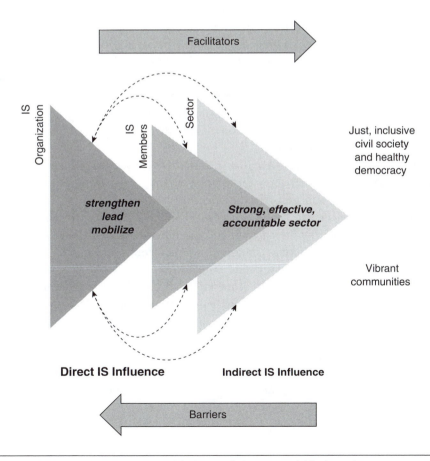

Figure 6.8   Independent Sector (IS) Theory of Change Model (Independent Sector, 2007)

this is shaded the darkest for emphasis. The indirect influences are those mediated by IS members on the sector as well as those mediated by the sector on communities and society. Lighter and lighter shading is used to show the changes in influence. This distinction is one way to communicate visually which of the outcomes and impact are closest to the work of the organization. Thin double-headed arrows are used to indicate an interactive and reciprocal feedback relationship with IS bridging members to sector to society.

When using models to design evaluations and evaluation systems with a relatively short time horizon, we suggest the use of direct and indirect influences. This device helps to keep the "do" and "get" relationship most tightly coupled. This way the later models can focus on those outcomes with the strongest and closest connection to those aspects with the highest strategic priority. The concept of enabling and disabling environmental issues is captured in the arrows labeled Facilitators and Barriers.

The IS program logic model (Figure 6.9) is read from left to right, and content is grouped in three areas relative to outcomes: emerging issues (Stronger Communities), operations (Stronger IS), and signature work (Stronger Nonprofits). The priority areas are included because they have special significance to staff. They reflect internal action plans and accountabilities. Outputs result from strategies in the priority areas (here a large number of activities are subsumed). They contribute to IS outcomes. The strength of communities (society), nonprofit organizations (members and the sector), and IS (the organization) are all linked to the outcomes named in the theory of change. This model displays the work of the entire membership organization, thus there is a wide variety of targets for outcomes (e.g., members, staff, policymakers, sector influentials). This model is used for monitoring (process side, outputs) and evaluation (outcomes). The intent is to be explicit and to show reflection processes for staff that connect data from each side to inform the work of the whole.

In this model, the ellipses are critical features that convey groups, flow, and relative (internal) value. They show the strands of work from strategies through to desired outcomes and impact. They intersect to show interaction and integration among program elements. The Priority Areas column is a custom element that is important for organizing information and meaning for those creating and using the model. The model describes "progress toward outcomes and impact" on the far right. It does not, intentionally, define time in months or years. Progress toward outcomes is used to indicate that a sequence of outcomes from awareness through to action is implied. The broad outcome statements are unpacked in detailed indicator and data collection tables not highlighted here. Arrows are not used. This is because of the highly interwoven nature of the organizations work across departments. All strategies contribute to all outcomes. The outputs and outcomes shown in this model draw on a variety of communication, policy advocacy, and individual behavior change theories. Resources, at the far left, are synonymous with inputs and are essential to the organization's work.

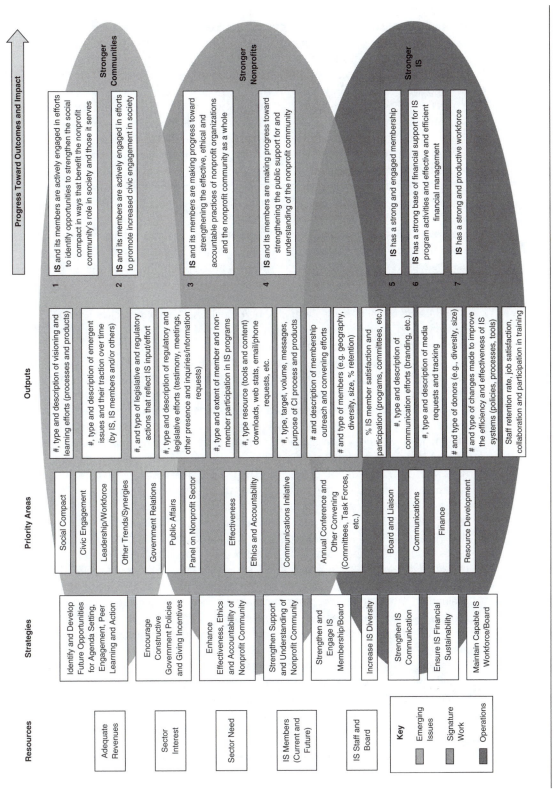

Figure 6.9 Independent Sector Program Logic Model (Independent Sector, 2007)

Independent Sector (IS) is a nonprofit, nonpartisan coalition of approximately 600 charities, foundations, and corporate philanthropy programs that collectively represent tens of thousands of charitable groups in every state across the nation. Its mission is to advance the common good by leading, strengthening, and mobilizing the nonprofit community.

As part of its commitment to continuous improvement, Independent Sector secured grant funds to design and implement an evaluation system prototype. The models discussed in this example are part of early efforts to develop an evaluation system that will meet selected formative and summative information needs of the organization.

To create a shared understanding about what could be included in an evaluation system, IS senior staff and an IS board member, with support from Phillips Wyatt Knowlton, Inc., created both a theory of change model and a program logic model. Both types of models were generated over several meetings with the staff, with modifications made as a result of subsequent discussions that clarified various aspects of the organization's work. Also important to the development of the models were the organization's strategic business plan and annual departmental work plans, as were the experiences and perspectives of staff.

Independent Sector's theory of change model displays its distinctive role in strengthening, leading, and mobilizing the nonprofit community. This role is designed to support a more effective, more accountable sector, which in turn can support a just, inclusive civil society, a healthy democracy, and vibrant communities. This theory of change model recognizes the direct influence of Independent Sector on its members and the nonprofit community as a whole; and by working through these organizations, the indirect influence IS has on the sector and society. Defining the ways in which IS can have influence helps to determine where to focus evaluation efforts so that the organization is assessing the areas with greater potential for direct influence. The model also recognizes the dynamic external environment in which IS operates, including the issues that facilitate the organization's efforts and the barriers that it faces.

IS's program logic model includes the organization's "priority areas" that reflect the focus of staff efforts. Much of the work of IS takes place across departments through integrated strategies and approaches. While logic models generally offer a sequence of short-, intermediate-, and long-term goals, the breadth and depth of IS work occurs on a far greater scale than can be captured with the limited resources available for this project. Rather than building the evaluation system around long-term goals, the logic model and the evaluation process show outcomes as indicators of progress, rather than on a set timeframe. Using this model, senior staff were able to focus the collection of evaluation data on selected outcomes. The priority areas that were selected for the initial focus of the pilot evaluation system were its work on public policy on behalf of the nonprofit community; providing leadership on ethics, accountability, and effectiveness; and building a strong membership base.

Prior to this project, Independent Sector had not formally used logic models, although several staff members were aware of them in other contexts. Staff found the graphic display to be useful in articulating the way the organization works, its goals, and intended outcomes. The models were also instrumental in underscoring the integrated nature of strategies, activities, and tasks among IS departments. Several strand models, displaying greater detail about a specific area (e.g., policy), were created to support inquiry and dialogue around monitoring.

Creating and using the models has contributed to building evaluation capacity with the staff as versions were built and combinations of elements were assembled and recast. The logic model provided a shared understanding of the organization's intended outcomes and how it works toward those outcomes. This, in turn, enabled external facilitators to explore and design an evaluation system that could ensure that the information gathered would be of use to IS management.

Questions

1. Is the level of detail in the theory of change model adequate to explain how change is expected to happen? Why or why not?

2. How would you draw a model representing the IS theory of change?

3. Are the relationships between the theory of change and program logic model evident? Why or why not?

4. What are the advantages and disadvantages of not specifying time in the program logic model outcomes?

5. Could you build action or project management plans from this program model? Why or why not?

6. Is there enough information to generate evaluation questions from the theory of change or program model?

7. Are the ellipses adequate in organizing the content, left to right, or is more detail about relationships between activities and outcomes necessary? Why or why not?

References

For more information about Independent Sector, see: http://www.independent sector.org

In Summary

Logic models describe and reflect thinking about programs. They are a display of information and the relationships among elements that depends largely on graphic presentation. In practice, logic models address a vast range of content areas and formats. Some are simple and others are complex. They are influenced by who creates them and their creators' culture. Sometimes models are used as templates to align and organize related work. The choices of elements used in a model are significant in their interpretation. Often, models are read left to right. Circular displays, top-to-bottom, and other orientations are increasingly common. This chapter offers examples of real-use models with considerable variation.

Learning Resources

Reflection

1. Is there consistent use of symbols and shapes in the case models? How do you ensure models are "read" or interpreted with the same meaning by everyone?

2. Does your field or workplace have technical or cultural standards for communicating that might influence your models?

3. What do the cases suggest about how models can be used to transfer and diffuse ideas? What challenges would an organization face using logic models as a communications tool? What benefits seem evident?

4. What do the cases suggest about the use of logic models in the context of measurement? How can models support measurement and evaluation?

5. Which applications are most like and most different from your current use of models? How? Why?

Exercises

1. Select a case and conduct a "mark up" (see Chapter 4). What changes would you make? Why? Compare the model you create with versions created by colleagues. Discuss your differences. Which model do you think is the best and why?

2. Divide the cases in this chapter among your colleagues and contribute your analysis to the matrix below:

Case and Model	Display Features	Use	Creators, Process	Other

Once this matrix is completed, discuss the variation among models. Which feature choices might work best under what conditions?

3. Select a theory of change model from the cases and apply the suggestions we offer in Chapter 2. How would the model change?

4. Select a program logic model from the cases and apply the modeling suggestions we offer in Chapter 4. How would the model change?

5. With your colleagues, list the stakeholders in any case you choose. Then, independently, cite with whom and what action steps you would use to generate a program logic model. Compare and contrast your list of stakeholders and sequence of steps with others. What rationales are used to explain differences?

References and Supplemental Readings

Texts

Buzan, T. (2002). *How to mind map: The thinking tool that will change your life.* New York: Thorsons/HarperCollins.

Craig, M. (2003). *Thinking visually: Business applications of 14 core diagrams.* New York: Continuum

Lohr, L. L. (2003). *Creating graphics for learning and performance: Lessons in visual literacy.* Upper Saddle River, NJ: Pearson Education.

Margulies, N. (2005). *Visual thinking: Tools for mapping your ideas.* Williston, VT: Crown House.

Nast, J. (2006). *Idea mapping: How to access your hidden brain power.* New York: John Wiley.

Racine, N. J. (2002). *Visual communication: Understanding maps, charts, diagrams and schematics.* New York: Learning Express.

Other Resources

In addition to the other modeling resources cited in Chapters 1 through 5, see:

Logical Frameworks (Logframes)

Asian-Initiative. (n.d.). *The logical framework for planning, monitoring and evaluation.* Retrieved February 15, 2008, from http://www.asia-initaitive.org/pdfs/chapter5.pdf

Food and Agriculture Organization of the United Nations. (1999). *Manual on logframes within the CGIAR system.* Retrieved February 15, 2008, from http://www.fao.org/wair docs/TAC/X5747E/x5747e00.HTM

International Labour Office. (2006). *ILO technical cooperation manual: Development cooperation.* Version 1. Geneva: Author.

Causal Loop Diagrams

Maani, K. E., & Cavan, R. Y. (2002). *Systems thinking and modeling: Understanding change and complexity.* Auckland, NZ: Prentice Hall/Pearson Education.

Pegasus Communications. (2004). *Causal loop diagrams.* Retrieved February 15, 2008, from http://www.pegasuscom.com/cld.html

Williams, R., & Imam, I. (2006). *Systems concepts in evaluation.* Battle Creek, MI: W. K. Kellogg Foundation. Retrieved October 25, 2007, from http://www.wkkf.org/DesktopModules/ WKF.00_DmaSupport/ViewDoc.aspx?fld=PDFFile&CID=281&ListID=28&ItemID= 5000253&LanguageID=0

Note

1. The David and Lucile Packard Foundation is a tax-exempt charitable organization qualified under section 501(c)(3) and classified as a private foundation under section 509(a) of the Internal Revenue Code. Packard Foundation funds may be used to support some, but not all, of the activities of grantees and others described in this logic model. No Packard Foundation funds are used to support or oppose any candidate for election to public office. No Packard Foundation funds are "earmarked" or designated to be used for lobbying or "attempts to influence legislation" (as defined in section 4945(d)(1) of the Internal Revenue Code).

CHAPTER 7

Exploring Archetypes

This chapter suggests readers consider the potent value archetypes can give to their own models. Archetypes are a tested, general template for an intervention, program, or strategy. Often, with modification, they can inform your planning, evaluation, communication, or other needs. Archetypes can also provoke new thinking and provide a quality check that improves ideas.

Learner Objectives

- Describe the rationale for evidence-based models
- Define a logic model archetype
- Specify contributions an archetype can make to modeling
- Name the limitations of archetypes

Why squander the knowledge we have about what works? Many important services, products, and programs have been built on the good efforts of others. For example, while automakers may change body styles year to year, they repeat great headlight designs that are cost efficient, aesthetic, and effective. Software programmers do this too. Once a particular code path is created that works well, it is often repeated as part of a subsequent routine. These examples demonstrate good use of prior knowledge with a highly positive effort to value (efficiency) and impact (effectiveness) ratio. Theory of change and program logic models can garner some of these benefits by using archetypes. They offer a substantive contrast to trial and error. Because archetypes are evidence based and tested, they can help jumpstart your modeling.

The Blank Page Challenge

As you start to think about how your planned work and intended results might look on paper, a blank page sometimes feels like a steep challenge. In many cases, there is no need to start with a blank page. Archetypes are a great remedy for "model block" or "display paralysis." In addition to getting some shapes and words on paper, they can also contribute significantly to model quality.

We define archetypes as commonly used templates that offer simple evidence-based guides for action. An archetype often looks and feels just like a theory of change or a program logic model. The main difference between an archetype and a logic model is that the elements, relationships, and outcomes specified in the archetype are tested or proven. They are grounded in research and/or evaluation that specifically confirms the validity of the connections as drawn. We touched on the concept behind archetypes in earlier chapters when we emphasized the importance of grounding your models in evidence. In this chapter, we take the next step by sharing some examples.

It is very likely that models relevant to your needs are already drawn and available on the Internet, in books, or in journal articles. You might pick simple archetypes from several bodies of research and combine them to create an initial version of a theory of change or program logic model. Or you might find a model and use it in its entirety with only some minor changes. Archetypes can model any number of broad strategies to results pathways and illustrate the detailed connections between activities and outcomes. They can display common functions like collaboration, communication, advocacy, professional development, sustainability, and a whole range of other topics. They can be general or discipline specific (e.g., health, education, public administration, environment).

For example, three of the cases in Chapter 6 show models built on archetypes. The Preschool, Sustainable Living, and Renewable Energy examples are clear about the underlying evidence their programs and/or models are built upon. Rather than invent a policy change initiative totally from scratch, the Packard Foundation used Kingdon's policy stream theory, and the body of research behind it, as a theory of change to guide their program design and its evaluation. Similarly, in the Energy example, Roger's diffusion of innovations research was used. The Energy and Sustainable Living examples show how a common overarching program framework can be used as a starting point for the development of project-specific logics. Although in this chapter we encourage readers to build on the evidence-based models already available, you may find the need to delve deeper into the literature to create your own.

Archetypes can provide a framework for content that is revised to suit your distinct context or used "as is" because they are already diagrams that are proven to work. The features of a logic model archetype vary just as theory of change and program models do (see Chapter 1). Evaluation logic models can also be archetypes. These models focus their content on measurement. They specify outcomes as well as indicators and often data collection tools that offer optimal points for evaluative inquiry, whether formative or summative.

Archetypes and Learning

In Chapter 6, we offered diversity in display as a rich field for learning. This chapter suggests archetypes have considerable value, too. Archetypes might be thought of as recipes. For instance, a tried-and-true recipe for banana bread passed on through generations always delivers great-tasting banana bread. Carefully following the inputs and directions of a particular recipe that is well proven or improved through frequent use can provide sure results. Archetypes are like recipes in that they rely on a measurable, proven set of ingredients. Execution of the recipe means results are predictable. Someone just learning to cook might choose to follow a recipe exactly, but later might "experiment" more with the ingredients or the sequence of steps.

As a "jumpstart" for your work, archetypes fill a blank page and identify the elements and conditions that might be modified. Building on the banana bread example, as most bakers know, recipes for banana bread can vary slightly depending on both conditions and preferences. Any given recipe for banana bread may require a different temperature depending on the pan size or material or oven type. And, if you like nuts or chocolate—those additions might be positive innovations too. Sometimes dietary restrictions or allergies require substitutions. While it is possible to have minor distinctions reflecting skills or preferences, a recipe identifies inputs and activities to secure the intended result. Likewise, it is possible to use experience and evidence to "improve" a recipe. These variations in the recipe are still results-focused, they just respond to different palates. In real-world execution, a program or change effort recipe can vary because of many internal or external conditions (e.g., budget constraints, culture, skills, and staff).

Recipes for Change

Earlier, we described knowledge and assumptions as important quality features for logic models. Similarly, archetypes rely on theory first and are then substantiated by research and evaluation. They use evidence as the basis for their recipe. Like reliable recipes, archetypes can support replication and, in that sense, they can be used prescriptively. Alternatively, they can also support innovation by providing a grounded but initial platform to generate new ideas. And archetypes offer greater chances of success under a variety of conditions because of this reliability.

One area where archetypes could be particularly helpful is in planning for and evaluating the vast number of programs and efforts that target the actions of individuals and organizations. For example, there are many theories of how and why individuals change the behavior that program staff and evaluators often use (e.g., Stretcher and Rosenstock's health belief model, Itzak's theory of planned behavior, or Prochaska and DiClemente's stages and processes of self-change; see Supplemental Readings at the end of the chapter). Although these theories are not described in detail here, they may be helpful to your work and do inform some of the examples we have selected for this chapter and those in Chapter 6. They are just a few pieces of relevant research that can be useful in identifying, creating, or using archetypes aimed at planning for or evaluating behavior change.

We often use the early work of Claude Bennett as a starting point to build models that include individual behavior change as outcomes. Bennett's approach, now widely known as TOP (targeting outcomes of programs) focuses on the outcomes in planning, implementing, and evaluating programs. Notably, TOP models generally show how individual change occurs. Although he created them more than 30 years ago, Bennett articulated specific steps in change that help us focus on those aspects of a program most closely related to effectiveness—whether the change effort is among individuals, groups, or organizations. We see threads of Bennett's work in many of the models used as examples here and those we see in our practice. It was using his simple recipe to inform our models that gave rise to our thinking that similar archetypes could be found or created for other content. Theoretical concepts, determined and tested through research, can inform the content in your models.

Value of Archetypes

Archetypes, just like recipes, are important because if the same model is repeatedly implemented, it can be used as a platform to inform learning about how to improve implementation and results. This means we can work toward precision so that when replication of results is sought—it is a real possibility. Further, we can also "stand on the shoulders" of the good work done before us and have it inform where we might improve a process or result. In effect, this serves the development of knowledge. Several mature fields, specifically health and education, have archetypes that practitioners rely on because of their proven, well-established content. It is more likely, in some situations, to get the results sought by using an archetype already developed and tested than starting from scratch.

In general, the archetype examples selected for this chapter serve either individual/group change or communities and systems change. Archetypes can contribute to both program planning and evaluation as they generate new learning about intentional variations in their content or execution. When program efforts require shared elements or evaluation needs to aggregate impact, archetypes can provide an umbrella or framework for design. Often, evaluation archetypes are linked to valid and reliable measures.

More Critical Thinking

Archetypes can provide substantial benefits because they are founded on evidence and prior research. They can launch your own models by capitalizing on prior testing and experience. Even so, archetypes are no substitute for critical thinking that generates appropriate revisions. Critical thinking is a key contributor to logic models because it employs intellectual criteria like clarity, credibility, relevance, and significance. It helps models (and consequently what is modeled) because it requires analysis and evaluation, and it restructures thought patterns. We believe that it is important to avoid the risk of actions based on flawed or false premises. Critical thinking helps form judgments that reconcile evidence with good sense and innovation. Archetypes are valuable to be aware of and use, but it is still important to employ some of the quality steps we have suggested previously. We provide extensive description of processes that engage critical thinking in Chapter 4. Critical thinking can contribute substantially to strategy development.

Selected Archetype Examples

The following archetype examples are drawn from a range of disciplines: social science, health care, communication, management, and government. Some aim at individual and group change, while others tackle communities and systems. We think they offer an interesting view of how experts/stakeholders describe their recipes for change. In each example, we introduce the model and then we provide some context about its use. References for each example are also included. The health promotion and organizational effectiveness examples include several models we consider archetypes.

We hope that individually and together these archetypes are useful for solving your blank-page paralysis. More important, they represent the rich possibilities of existing models and the valuable contributions archetypes can make to your efforts. As in prior chapters, a resources section after the examples can be used to support additional learning. For this chapter, it includes a short compendium of related text, journal, and Internet materials that is organized by topic and is placed after the reflection and exercises.

Example 1: Federal Block Grants

Juvenile Justice and Delinquency Prevention

Reading from left to right, the Juvenile Accountability Block Grant (JABG) Logic Model (Figure 7.1) begins on the far left with problem and sub-problem(s) columns. This model illustrates an initiative targeting the improvement of system and program accountability as well as performance improvement as solutions to the delinquency problem.

The top right side of the model shows how the federal program wants its grantees to describe and measure types of efforts at the system and program levels as well as how to quantify results (mandatory rectangles within large downward pointing arrows). At the system level, the JABG model shows the relationship between types of system improvements (staff, infrastructure, and training) and grant funds invested with number of programs, length of service, and the use of graduated sanctions and best practices. These are noted as being of particular importance in influencing rates of participating youth who reoffend. At the direct service program level, the model shows the relationship between the implementation of youth programs, the number of youth served using graduated sanctions, completion of program requirements, and the rate at which participating youth repeat offending.

Federal Juvenile Accountability Block Grant (JABG) Logic Model

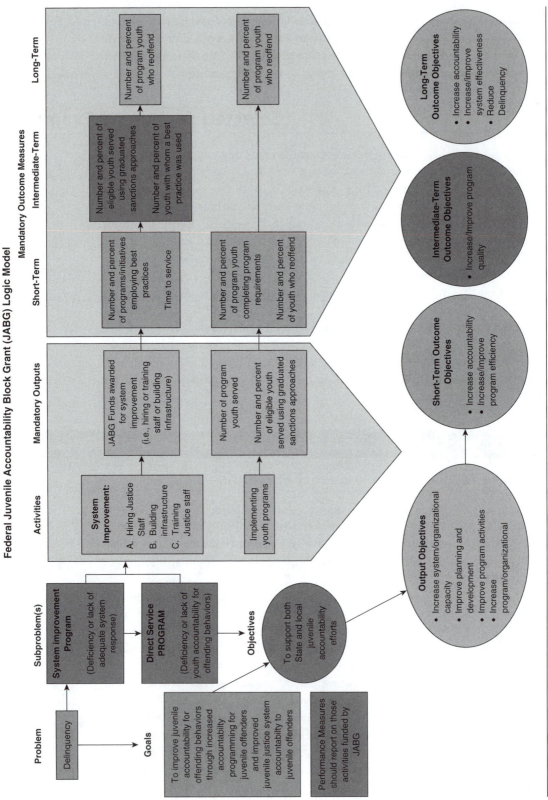

Figure 7.1 Juvenile Accountability Block Grant Logic Model

SOURCE: U.S. Office of Juvenile Justice and Delinquency Prevention, 1997

It also specifies an objectives pathway (ovals, bottom right). Although this is not frequently seen in models, it serves the purpose here to show how the mandated output and outcomes measures provide evidence of improved programs and systems in terms of specific and measurable accomplishments such as capacities, accountability, efficiency, quality, and effectiveness.

The Office of Juvenile Justice and Delinquency Prevention (OJJDP) competitively distributes federal funding to community and regional nonprofit organizations. In OJJDP grant solicitations, logic models are required as a key element of funding proposals. They are consistent with both the Government Performance and Results Act of 1993 (GPRA) and the Program Assessment Rating Tool (PART). While the models help explain program design, they are specifically intended to help applicants select relevant performance measures. The OJJDP encourages grant applicants to use its designated generic logic model as a template to create a logic model for applicants' customized program. OJJDP staff encourage the use of the template to ensure the applicant's goals correspond to those identified at OJJDP, determine the program and purpose areas for appropriate assignment, and select indicators that will show required performance data. In all, this Office has more than two dozen programs with logic models and associated indicators for grantees to use.

The model in Figure 7.1 is tied to specific performance measures named in the block grants program. They include but are not limited to graduated sanctions, training, juvenile records system, information sharing, accountability, risk and needs assessment, school safety, restorative justice, probation, and others. The Juvenile Accountability Block Grant (JABC) model and its clear performance measures are aligned with the specifications laid out in the OJJDP generic logic model template. In this way, the OJJDP offers grantees some important tools that support effectiveness. While not every program model proposal will be the same, they must include elements of a change prescription that secures specified outcomes all aimed at reducing delinquency and improving juvenile justice.

If content specific to Juvenile Justice were removed, this model could be a generic recipe for a grant proposal on any subject or change agenda. The elements of the model (e.g., outcomes, goals, objectives, activities, and outputs) are common features of any intervention program. It is especially helpful that the model encourages identification of both the problem and the sub-problems to be addressed through appropriate activities. If you were planning, managing, or evaluating programs in this content area, the supplementary materials and more detailed logic models (specific to particular programs) provided on the OJJDP Web site would help focus and stimulate your thinking.

References

For additional information and more resources about the OJJDP work with logic models, see:

Developing a logic model. (n.d.). Retrieved October 25, 2007, from http://ojjdp.ncjrs.gov/grantees/pm/logic_models.html

The JABG logic model. (n.d.). Retrieved October 25, 2007, from http://ojjdp.ncjrs.org/grantees/ pm/solicitations/2006/jabg06logicmodel.pdf and related page views.

The OJJDP generic logic model. (n.d.) Retrieved October 25, 2007, from http://ojjdp.ncjrs.org/grantees/pm/generic_logic_model.pdf

Performance measures for the JABG program. (n.d.). Retrieved October 25, 2007, from http://ojjdp.ncjrs.org/grantees/pm/2007/jabgp.html

Logic models and performance measures for title V formula grants. (n.d.). Retrieved October 25, 2007, from http://www.dsgonline.com/program_logic_model/titlev_pm.htm

Example 2: Pathways Mapping Initiative (PMI)

Education Readiness and Success

This model (called a "map" by its authors) describes the most critical actions and goals that are proven to contribute to student success in the third grade. This model is read both left to right and top to bottom. Goals, specified in a numbered sequence from top to bottom, are cited for individual children in the context of a community. Each of the six goals contributes to third grade success (far right). Several evidence-based categories of actions for each goal are also specified. Indicators of third grade success are listed. This model shows the comprehensive systems view from which programs or groups of programs might approach their work.

Assembling the best information from a wide array of resources across diverse systems and disciplines is central to the approach used in the Pathways Mapping Initiative (PMI). The PMI is an initiative of the Project on Effective Interventions at Harvard University, funded by the Annie E. Casey and W. K. Kellogg Foundations. The PMI tackles several concerns and what works in America's families and neighborhoods. The PMI has assembled a broad and deep knowledge pool on selected issues. Through a process they call "mental mapping," the PMI "systematically applies reasonable judgments and plausible interpretations" to evidence culled from experience, theory, and evaluation findings. It is a knowledge management project aimed at effectiveness.

The Ready for School and Succeeding at Third Grade map covers content about school readiness. Each component is discussed and detail is provided on the actions with examples, indicators of progress, elements of effective implementation, rationale, and research evidence. This and other PMI models are very comprehensive because of the quantity and quality of materials "behind" them. It relies on knowledge to inform elements, assemble the general recipe, and direct users to viable options that reflect their context to complete a customized model. At its Web site, click-through content for each area of the map is accessible so that users can create a map that reflects their own community conditions and circumstances.

Few other archetypes have this support in the breadth and quality of content for each feature. This, as well as the rationale, indicators, and attributes are also distinct and substantially enhance the archetypes' value. Consistent with logic models, the Ready for School map has tremendous utility for many tasks. It can help with assessment or planning for a school improvement effort, inform proposals, and identify examples of effective strategies.

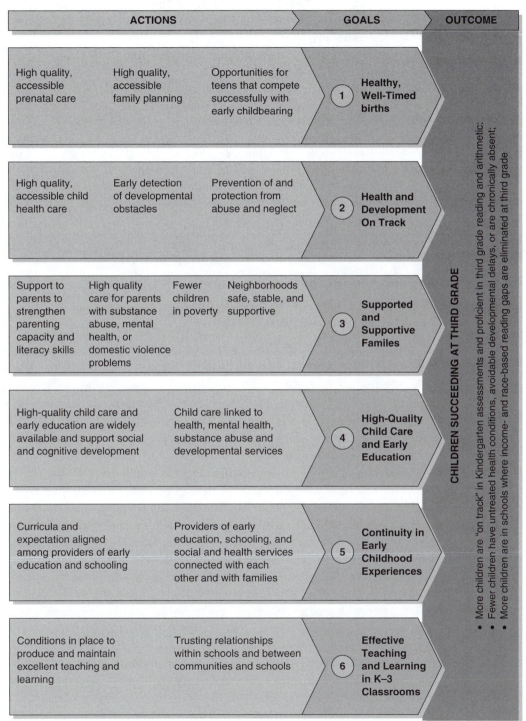

**Actions Overview, Pathway to Children
Ready for School and Succeeding at Third Grade**

Figure 7.2   Ready for School and Succeeding at Third Grade

SOURCE: U.S. Pathways Mapping Initiative, 2007.

References

In addition to School Readiness, PMI offers pathway maps and other materials for successful young adulthood, family economic success, and the prevention of child abuse and neglect.

For additional information and more resources about the PMI see: http://www.pathwasystooutcomes.org as well as

How to use the FES pathway. (n.d.). Retrieved October 25, 2007, from http://www.path waystooutcomes.org/index.cfm?fuseaction=Page.viewPage&pageID=548

Succeeding at third grade model. (n.d.). Retrieved October 25, 2007, from http://www .pathwaystooutcomes.org/_uploads/documents/live/3RDGRADEPATHWAYPDF8-15-07 .pdf

Schorr, L. B., & Marchand, V. (2007). *Pathway to children ready for school and succeeding at third grade.* Washington, DC: Pathways Mapping Initiative, Project on Effective Intervention.

Example 3: Public Health

Generic Model for Planning and Evaluating Health Promotion and the Interactive Domain Model

Although nearly a decade has passed since its creation, the Generic Planning and Evaluating Health Promotion Model (Figure 7.3) is a comprehensive archetype with current relevance because it can support a whole system for planning, implementing, and evaluating (Goodstadt, 1999). This model is read from top to bottom. It begins with the end in mind—human potential and reduced health and social costs—and maps to the types of activities that are known to contribute to achieving these desired ends.

It illustrates in a three-column outline form not only many of the elements important to consider when planning, managing, and evaluating this type of program but also the complex nature of the relationships among elements. The left-hand column, labeled Evaluation Loop, serves as the key to the types of information in the rows in the central section from top to bottom. The right-hand column points out that the top half of the model illustrates the main content for health promotion programs and the bottom half focuses on building specific initiatives based on this foundation. These outer layers describe features for evaluation that are integrated with program planning. The central portion shows content areas.

At the top of the central portion, overall impacts and health promotion goals are named. The central portion of the model presents specified health promotion values, mechanisms, and prerequisites. These are important features to consider in that they provide the principles by which programs should operate and identify features that may present barriers or facilitators to success.

Below these grounding statements, the model points out that health promotion action can target and thus influence individuals, the community, and/or systems (e.g., environment, public policy, and services). These action areas contribute to

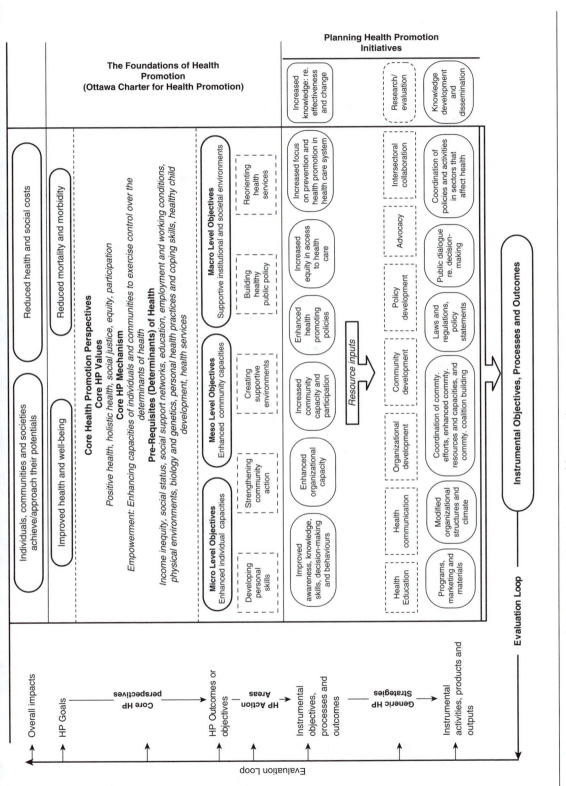

Figure 7.3 Generic Model for Planning and Evaluating Health Promotion

SOURCE: Goodstadt, 1999.

micro-, meso-, and macro-level objectives/outcomes that show the levels at which health programs may operate (dashed-line rectangles).

Then moving from the foundation section to the initiative section, the model illustrates specific program outcomes for individuals, communities, and systems (ovals). In turn, the outcomes are "fed" via resource inputs to connect to the range of generic strategies in health promotion that are known to produce them. They include health education, communication, organization, community and policy development, advocacy, and inter-sectoral collaboration. The last set of ovals identifies the broad categories of activities in each strategy a program could use, depending on the level they want to target (individuals, communities, system). It then infers that more specific objectives, processes, and outcomes would need to be specified for each selected activity.

This model also shows the places where evaluation could be placed to inform both the health promotion field/system and individual programs (left-hand column and the far, lower right column). The far, lower right column highlights that health promotion programs are served by the evaluation loop and that increased knowledge about effectiveness and change should be included as a strategy. This requires research/evaluation, knowledge development, and dissemination.

This generic model helps health promotion program planners, managers, and evaluators see the "big picture" and better understand where their programs fit and relate to other efforts. It shows that it takes initiatives at multiple levels to achieve the desired impact. This model was created by Michael Goodstadt, who is affiliated with the Centre for Health Promotion, Department of Public Health Sciences, University of Toronto (Canada). The thinking that is portrayed in this first model has evolved over time. In the next archetype, Kahan and Goodstadt show another way to harness the power of best practices to improve health promotion programs.

The second archetype model (Figure 7.4) in health promotion was revised recently. Its use in health promotion efforts is supported by the Centre for Health Promotion at the University of Toronto. They have used models for planning and evaluation for some time. The Interactive Domain Model (IDM) for Best Practices in Health Promotion was generated by a Best Practices Work Group associated with the Centre. Best practices in health promotion are those sets of processes and activities that are consistent with health promotion values, goals and ethics, theories, and evidence as well as those that are most likely to achieve health promotion goals in a given situation.

The IDM and its accompanying evidence-based framework have been tested in several Canadian communities with federal (Canadian) financial support. The IDM has contributed to positive results in a number of countries. There are comprehensive additional resources related to applying this model available on the Centre's Web site. In addition, there is software and a quality checklist available for download to support groups in exploring the model and its related measurement framework.

The IDM features three domains: Health Promotion Practice, Underpinnings of Best Practice, and Understanding of the Environment. Each of these domains has sub-areas and the features in them are carefully defined in the associated framework. The Underpinnings domain consists of what we have referred to as

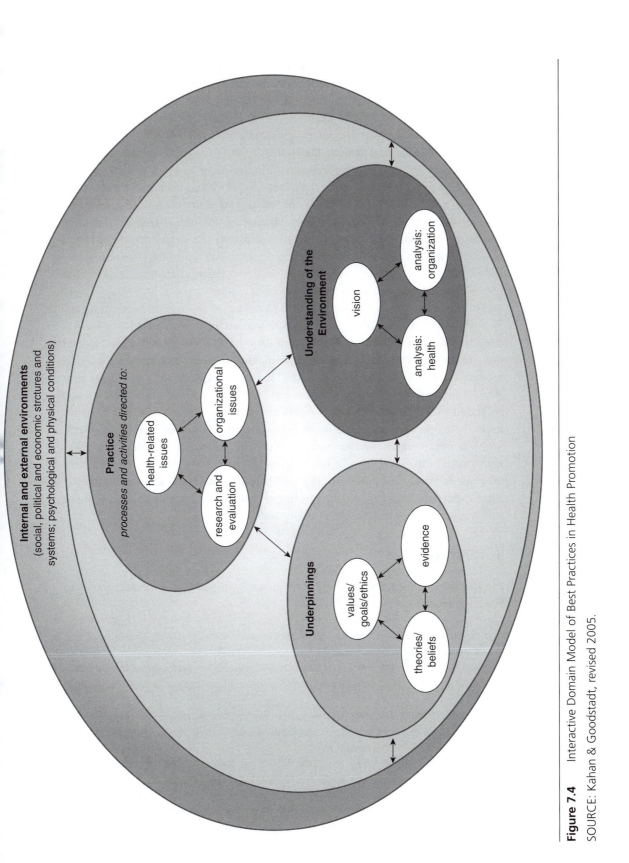

Figure 7.4   Interactive Domain Model of Best Practices in Health Promotion

SOURCE: Kahan & Goodstadt, revised 2005.

assumptions and evidence of plausibility (e.g., values, goals, ethics, theories/concepts, beliefs/assumptions, and evidence). This is much like the theory of change. The Understanding the Environment domain contains the organization/work vision and analysis, the health vision and analysis. This is similar to the activities and outcomes of the program logic model. The IDM adds an analysis of the current situation compared to the ideal to improve the ability to plan for greater feasibility. The Practice domain relates to what we refer to as an evaluation logic model. This domain examines the organizational/work and health responses to the situation and vision articulated by the other two domains and the research/evaluation component. The underlying premise of this model is that the quality and value of health promotion practice depends on the degree to which health professionals plan and implement their programs with sufficient attention to the IDM domains and sub-domains. It is the quality of the advance thinking, ongoing review, and revision that leads to better efforts.

These features interact and exist in broader internal and external environments. Similar to this text, the IDM supporting resources suggest questions to help process a series of steps that develop the content of the model. The IDM is designed to help those in the field charged with planning, managing, or evaluating health promotion projects from a best practices perspective. Kahan and Goodstadt assert that better efforts result when you first prepare the foundation for your action and then make an action plan that takes your resources and challenges into account. They have found best practices are viable when the processes and activities associated with health issues, research, and evaluation reflect the criteria and guiding principles represented in the IDM. They stress, as do we, the importance of consistency across the three domains. The authors of the IDM consider the IDM and its application as a multi-purpose "change" tool for practitioners and organizations who want to use a best practices approach to health promotion.

References

For additional information and more resources about the IDM of Best Practices in Health Promotion see:

Best practices in health promotion: The interactive domain model (IDM). (2007). Retrieved February 13, 2008, from http://www.bestpractices-healthpromotion.com

Goodstadt, M. (1999). *A generic model for planning and evaluating health promotion.* Retrieved May 7, 2008, from http://www.bestpractices-healthpromotion.com/coursereadings/id1.html

Goodstadt, M. (2007). *The use of logic models in health promotion practice.* Retrieved October 25, 2007, from http://www.goodworksonline.com/sitebuildercontent/sitebuilderfiles/webintroductiontologicmodels1.doc

Kahan, B., Groulx, D., & Wong, J. (2007). *Interactive Domain Model (IDM) best practices approach to better health: Follow-up to IDM use and impacts.* Centre for Health Promotion, University of Toronto. Retrieved May 6, 2008, from http://www.idmbestpractices.ca/pdf/IDM_follow-up_October2007_final.pdf

Kahan, B. & Goodstadt, M. (2001). The Interactive Domain Model of best practices in health promotion: Developing and implementing a best practices approach to health promotion. *Health Promotion Practice, 2*(1), 43–67.

Welcome to IDM best practices. (n.d.). Retrieved February 13, 2008, from http://www .idmbestpractices.ca/idm.php

Example 4: Organizational Effectiveness

Organizational Effectiveness for Advocacy

Policy advocacy is a popular focus of social change work and many foundations include it in their portfolio. In this example, we share two models that link an organizational effectiveness archetype with policy advocacy work. They were used together in a project to support evaluation efforts and now enable more effective design, planning, and implementation.

Another foundation, The California Endowment (TCE), has provided grants for policy and advocacy organizations for several years. These grants support grantees to advocate on a variety of issues, support organization infrastructure and staffing, and assist in communicating with policymakers. In an evaluation of this work, TCC Group drew upon a logic model they developed earlier that described an effective nonprofit organization as a starting point. The model, based on literature, was tested through some expert interviews and provides the capacities or organizational resources for an effective nonprofit organization. The assertion being that to be effective at policy advocacy, the nonprofit must first be an effective organization. This model is circular and the center ring of the circle focuses on four core capacities that an effective nonprofit organization must possess: leadership, adaptive, management, technical. It lists key aspects for each capacity. These capacities, in turn, influence organization culture (expressed by structure, rituals, history, language, beliefs, and values). These would serve as the outcomes of a capacity building initiative, for example.

The middle ring of the model lists the key resources needed to achieve organizational effectiveness. These include facilities, human resources, technology, program design/model, finances/funding, and time. The outer ring of the model illustrates the influence of the external environment on organizational capacity.

A model such as this serves as an archetype for organizational effectiveness and could be used to plan, implement, or evaluate programs targeting organizational capacity. The report cited in the References section includes the literature and research framework and evidence for the model as well as indicators and other materials.

The research-based features of the Organizational Effectiveness Model (Figure 7.5) became the assumptions upon which the subsequent advocacy model (Figure 7.6) was created. It is a blend of what we have referred to as theory of change and program logic models. It shows more detail than a basic theory of change but less than a full program logic model (activities for each strategy are not listed). The Advocacy Model is read from left to right; it starts with organizational capacities as defined

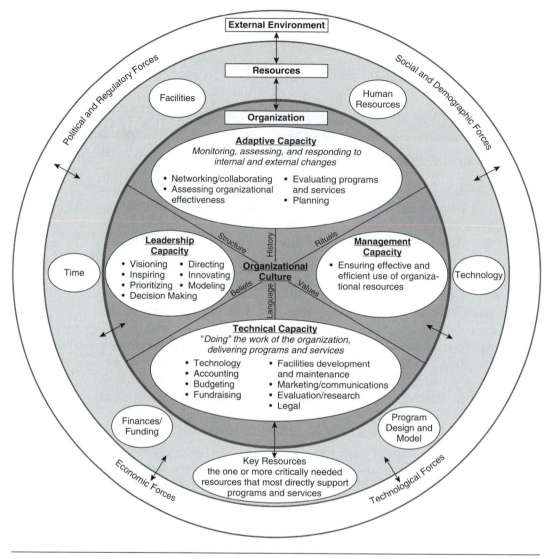

Figure 7.5   Organizational Effectiveness Model

SOURCE: TCC Group, 2003.

by the prior model. Advocacy organizations need to have sufficient adaptive, leadership, management, and technical capacities to do the work successfully. Then, it defines project inputs/resources, strategies, outcomes, and the impact.

The Outcome column should look familiar to readers in that it is consistent with the Kingdon policy stream theory of change used in the Preschool example in Chapter 6 (see Case 1). You can see the problem, proposal, and politics streams. Note also the dotted line from Outcomes back to Capacities. This indicates a feedback loop from evaluation of Outcomes back to the Organizational Resources. This reinforces program improvement by connecting progress toward outcomes with the capacity of the organization to accomplish them.

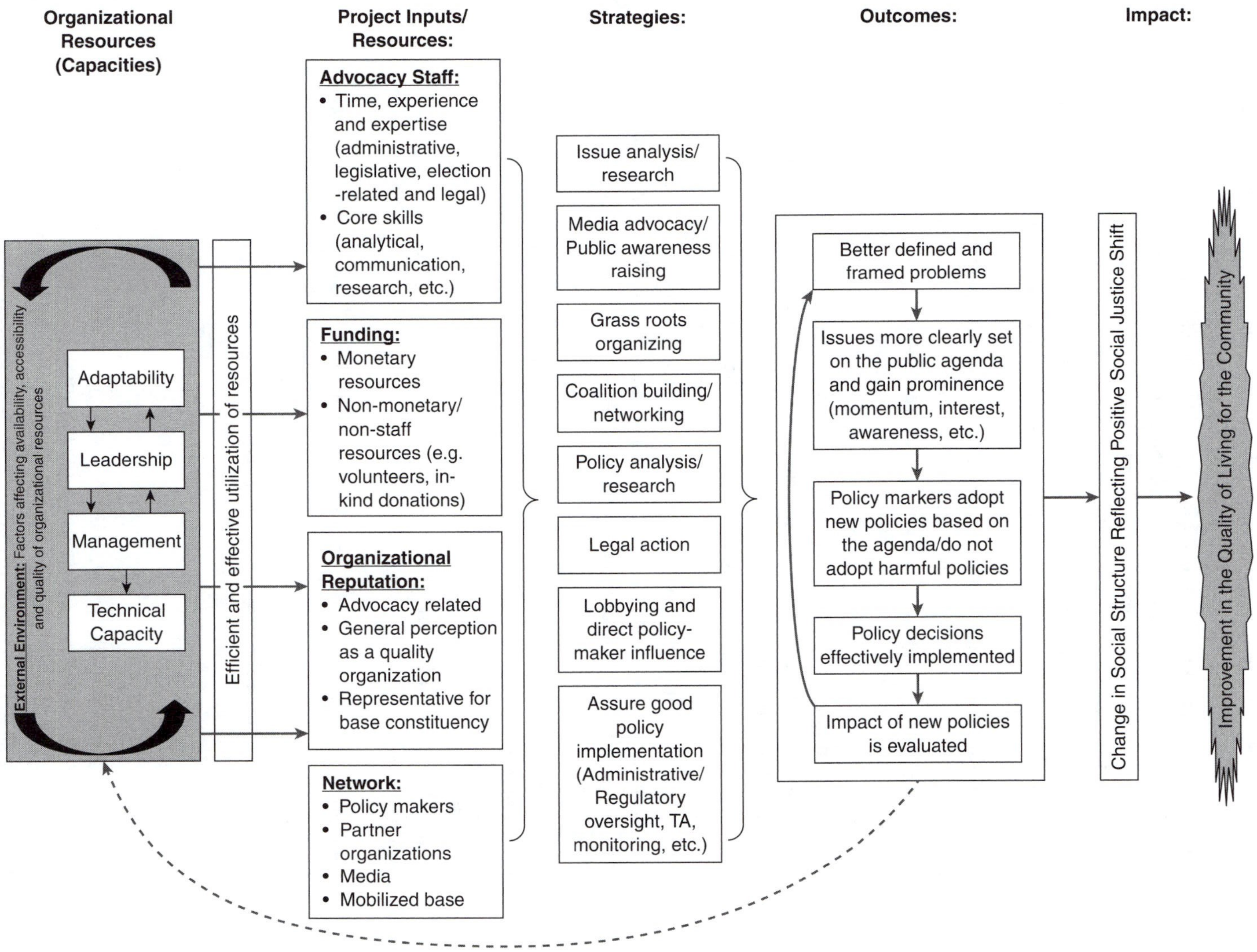
Organizational Resources (Capacities)
Project Inputs/ Resources:
Strategies:
Outcomes:
Impact:
External Environment: Factors affecting availability, accessibility and quality of organizational resources
Adaptability
Leadership
Management
Technical Capacity
Efficient and effective utilization of resources
Advocacy Staff:
• Time, experience and expertise (administrative, legislative, election -related and legal)
• Core skills (analytical, communication, research, etc.)
Funding:
• Monetary resources
• Non-monetary/ non-staff resources (e.g. volunteers, in-kind donations)
Organizational Reputation:
• Advocacy related
• General perception as a quality organization
• Representative for base constituency
Network:
• Policy makers
• Partner organizations
• Media
• Mobilized base
Issue analysis/ research
Media advocacy/ Public awareness raising
Grass roots organizing
Coalition building/ networking
Policy analysis/ research
Legal action
Lobbying and direct policy-maker influence
Assure good policy implementation (Administrative/ Regulatory oversight, TA, monitoring, etc.)
Better defined and framed problems
Issues more clearly set on the public agenda and gain prominence (momentum, interest, awareness, etc.)
Policy markers adopt new policies based on the agenda/do not adopt harmful policies
Policy decisions effectively implemented
Impact of new policies is evaluated
Change in Social Structure Reflecting Positive Social Justice Shift
Improvement in the Quality of Living for the Community

Figure 7.6 Logic Model for Advocacy Initiatives

SOURCE: The California Endowment and TCC Group, 2007.

TCC then developed several versions of an advocacy-specific capacity model that explicated the unique leadership, management, adaptive, and technical capacities needed to fully support an organization's policy and advocacy work. Because the California Endowment made general support grants to policy and advocacy organizations, the advocacy-specific capacity model became the evaluation framework for understanding if these grants made a difference.

Unlike direct service programs, policy and advocacy organizations must be able to change their strategy, and hence their policy and advocacy logic model, on a regular and frequent basis. This is in response to environmental/contextual changes and windows of opportunity, or to become more proactive toward the creation of environmental/systems change.

As such, the use of the program logic model as an evaluation framework is much more complicated when evaluating policy and advocacy work. It is for this reason, and that grants were general support rather than strategy specific, that the California Endowment and TCC decided that it would be more important to develop and evaluate the changes in organizational capacities that the grants affected in support of the policy and advocacy work that grantees implemented. The evaluation focused on the left hand side of the model (capacities and inputs columns) shown in Figure 7.6.

In this way, the logic model was a framework that connected the policy and advocacy strategy-to-outcome assumptions with the organizational effectiveness/ capacity assumptions for supporting the work. So, you can see how TCC Group used an archetype to create a logic model. This model could be used to plan, manage, or evaluate organizational readiness for advocacy as well as progress against advocacy outcomes.

References

For additional information about these models and the related evaluation project, contact Astrid Hendricks at The California Endowment or Peter York at TCC Group.

Coffman, J. (2007). Evaluation based on theories of the policy process. *Evaluation Exchange, 13*(1), 6–7.
Connelly, P. (2007). *Deeper capacity building for greater impact.* New York: TCC. Retrieved October 25, 2007, from http://www.tccgrp.com/pubs/capacity.php

In Summary

As tested, general templates for action, archetypes have great potential for informing your work. They can test the quality of your original efforts and generate new thinking. Archetypes are evidence based so they can reliably jumpstart your modeling. Archetypes can be thought of as recipes. They can contribute to planning, managing, and evaluation. They are improved upon by your own knowledge and experience because of your unique context and conditions. The breadth of content in an archetype varies. They look different and are often not referred to specifically as theories of change or logic models. What is important is that they contain the information needed to illustrate the basic concepts in theories of change or program logic models. Some represent a single strategy while others cover complex projects. This chapter provided examples of archetypal theory of change and program logic models.

Learning Resources

Reflection

1. In the absence of an archetype, what elements of knowledge can help you "jumpstart" creation of a logic model?

2. Does your field or discipline rely on any archetypes? If so, are some better than others? Why?

3. Name any challenges you might experience with using an archetype. Why could or would an archetype "fail"?

Exercises

1. Go to the Juvenile Justice Web site and prepare a program logic model. Compare and contrast with others who do the same. Was there fidelity to the template? Why? Why not? Select a model and discuss how it might be evaluated.

2. Find or create a description for a health care promotion program. Compare it to the IDM model or the earlier model Goodstadt built in Figure 7.3. What is the same and what is different? How would you change the program to align with one or the other archetype?

3. Locate a case study on policy development. Apply Kingdon's model to it. Does the model reflect the case you located? If not, why not?

4. Locate logic models for collaboration, sustainability, or marketing. Would they qualify as archetypes? How can they be used in your work?

References and Supplemental Readings

For this chapter, additional texts, journals, and Internet resources (when available) are organized relative to the subject matter content of the examples cited. This list is illustrative but not comprehensive. Many more resources exist than are cited here.

Evidence-Based Models

Baruch, G., Fonagy, P., & Robins, D. (2007). *Reaching the hard to reach: Evidence-based funding priorities for intervention and research.* New York: John Wiley.

Bennett, C. (1975). Up the hierarchy. *Journal of Extension, 13*(2), 7–12.

Blueprints for violence prevention. (2004). Retrieved October 25, 2007, from http://www.colorado.edu/cspv/blueprints/index.html

Centers for Disease Control and Prevention. (n.d.). *HIV/AIDS Prevention Research Synthesis (PRS) project.* Retrieved October 25, 2007, from http://www.cdc.gov/hiv/topics/research/prs/index.htm

Coalition for Evidence-Based Policy. (2003). *Identifying and implementing educational practices supported by rigorous evidence: A user friendly guide.* Washington, DC: Author. Retrieved October 25, 2007, from http://www.ed.gov/rschstat/research/pubs/rigorousevid/index.html

Department of Health and Human Services. (2007). *Identifying and selecting evidence-based interventions: Guidance document for the Strategic Prevention Framework State Incentive Grant Program.* Washington, DC: Substance Abuse and Mental Health Services Administration. Retrieved October 25, 2007, from http://captus.samhsa.gov/western/resources/prevmat/documents/Evidence-Based_CSAP_Guidance_Doc_1.07.pdf

Duignan, P. (2004). *Principles of outcome hierarchies: Contribution towards a general analytical framework for outcomes systems (outcomes theory).* A working paper. Retrieved May 7, 2008, from http://www.strategicevaluation.info/documents/122pdf.PDF

Norcross, J. C., Beutler, L. E., & Levant, R. F. (2006). *Evidence-based practices in mental health: Debate and dialogue on the fundamental questions.* Washington, DC: American Psychological Association.

Promising Practices Network on Children, Families and Communities. (2008). Retrieved October 25, 2007, from http://www.promisingpractices.net/

Proven models. (2008). Retrieved February 11, 2008, from http://www.provenmodels.com

Individual Change Models

Itzak, A. (1991). The theory of planned behavior. *Organizational Behavior and Human Decision Processes, 50,* 179–211.

Prochaska, J., & DiClemente, C. C. (1983). Stages and processes of self-change of smoking: Toward an integrative model of change. *Journal of Consulting and Clinical Psychology, 51,* 390–395.

Stretcher, V., & Rosenstock, I. (1997). The health belief model. In K. Glanz, F. M. Lewis, & B. Rimer (Eds.), *Health behavior and health education: Theory, research and practice* (2nd ed.). San Francisco, CA: Jossey-Bass.

Federal Accountability

Assessing program performance. (n.d.). Retrieved October 25, 2007, from http://www.whitehouse.gov/omb/part/index.html

Performance measurement challenges and strategies. (2003). Retrieved October 25, 2007, from http://www.whitehouse.gov/omb/part/challenges_strategies.html

Pathways Mapping Initiative

Mental mapping as a tool for improving community outcomes. (n.d.). Retrieved October 25, 2007, from http://www.pathwaystooutcomes.org/index.cfm?fuseaction=Page.viewPage&pageID=691

Schorr, L. B. (n.d.). *The Pathways Mapping Initiative in depth: A message from the director, Lisbeth B. Schorr.* Retrieved October 25, 2007, from http://www.pathwaystooutcomes .org/index.cfm?fuseaction=Page.viewPage&pageID=698

Schorr, L. B. (1989). *Within our reach: Breaking the cycle of disadvantage.* New York: Anchor/Random House.

Schorr, L. B. (1998). *Common purpose: Strengthening families and neighborhoods to rebuild America.* New York: Anchor/Random House.

Schorr, L. B. (2003). *Determining "what works" in social programs and social policies: Toward a more inclusive knowledge base.* Retrieved May 7, 2008, from http://www.brookings .edu/papers/2003/0226poverty_schorr.aspx

Health Promotion Practices

Bartholomew, L. K., Parcel, G. S., Kok, G., & Gottleib, N. H. (2006). *Planning health promotion programs: Intervention mapping* (2nd ed.). San Francisco: John Wiley.

Evidence based health promotion. (2008). Retrieved October 25, 2007, from http://www .health.vic.gov.au/healthpromotion/quality/evidence_index.htm

Lucas, K., & Lloyd, B. (2005). *Health promotion: Evidence and experience.* Thousand Oaks, CA: Sage.

McDonald, P. (2007). From evidence-based practice making to practice-based evidence making. *Health Promotion Practice, 8*(2), 140–144.

The pathway to evidence-based resources. (2008). Retrieved May 7, 2008, from http://library .umassmed.edu/ebpph/

Rychetnik, L., & Wise, M. (2004). Advocating evidence-based health promotion: Reflections and a way forward. *Health Promotion International, 19*(2), 247–257. Retrieved May 7, 2008, from http://heapro.oxfordjournals.org/cgi/content/full/19/2/247

Strategies for making your program "evidence-based." (2006). Retrieved October 25, 2007, from http://www.asaging.org/cdc/module7/phase5/index.cfm

Policy and Advocacy

Coffman, J. (n.d.). *Advocacy progress planner: An advocacy and policy change composite logic model.* Retrieved October 25, 2007, from http://planning.continuousprogress.org/

Guthrie, K., Louie, J., David, T., & Foster, C. (2005). *The challenge of assessing policy and advocacy initiatives: Part I. Strategies for a prospective evaluation approach.* Woodland Hills, CA: The California Endowment. Retrieved October 25, 2007, from http://www .calendow.org/uploadedFiles/Publications/Evaluation/challenge_assessing_policy _advocacy.pdf

Guthrie, K., Louie, J., & Foster, C. (2006). *The challenge of assessing policy and advocacy initiatives: Part II. Moving from theory to practice.* Woodland Hills, CA: The California Endowment. Retrieved October 25, 2007, from http://www.calendow.org/uploadedFiles/ challenge_assessing_policy_advocacy2.pdf

Innovation Network's advocacy evaluation project and resource center. (2008). [Requires free registration with Point K for access.] Retrieved October 25, 2007, from http://www.innonet.org/index.php?section_id=101&content_id=4

Sabatier, P. A. (2007). *Theories of the policy process* (2nd ed.). Boulder, CO: Westview.

Name Index

Alberta Heritage Foundation for Medical Research, 104
Annie E. Casey Foundation, 128
Australian Sustainable Living Program, 91

Bakersfield College, 107–109
Barrington, Gail, xiii
Barrington Research Group, Inc. 105
Bennett, Claude, 6, 15, 124
Berkowitz, Gale, xiii

Canadian Studentship Program, 104
Centre for Health Promotion at the University of Toronto, 132
Chen, Huey, 6, 15, 32
CLIPs (Communities of Learning, Inquiry, and Practice), 107–108, 109
Coffman, Julia, 93
Community Leadership Academy (CLA), 10, 20, 56–57, 73–74, 78, 79, 82–83
    Nonlinear Theory of Change Model, 29
    Outcome Indicators, 81
    Process Indicators, 79–80
    Program Evaluation Model, 11, 83–84
    Program Logic Model, 9, 78
    Theory of Change, 7–8, 74–75

David and Lucile Packard Foundation's Preschool for California's Children, 94–99, 122
Department of Environment and Conservation, 102, 122
DiClemente, C. C., 123

Fullan, Michael, 6, 15
Funnell, Sue C., 101

Goodstadt, Michael, 130–134
    Generic Planning and Evaluating Health Promotion Model, 130–132
    Interactive Domain Model (IDM), 132–134
Government Performance and Results Act of 1993 (GPRA), 127

Hardy, B., 103
Hendricks, Astrid, xiii
Hudson, B., 103

Independent Sector, 117,
    Program logic model, 114–116
    Theory of change model, 113–114
Innovologie, xiii
Insites, xiii
Itzak, A., 123

Jordan, Gretchen, B., xiii
Juvenile Accountability Block Grant (JABG) Logic Model, 125–127

Kahan, B., 133–134
Kingdon, John, 93–95, 122,
    Policy Stream Convergence, 93–95

Logic Model Development Guide, The, 7

Marchand, Vicky, xiii
Management by Objectives movement, 92
Measuring Program Outcomes, 6–7

National Science Foundation, 107

Our Environment—It's a Living Thing (OEILT), 101–103, 122

Parsons, Beverly, A., xiii
Prochaska, J., 123
Program Assessment Rating Tool (PART), 127
Program Evaluation Standards, 50
Program Improvement Pty., Ltd., xiii
Project on Effective Interventions, 128

Raynor, Jared, xiii
Reed, John, H., xiii
Reich, Kathleen, xiii
Rockey, Sherry, xiii
Rogers, P. J., 122
Rosenstock, I., 123

Salisbury, Lois, xiii
Sandia National Laboratories, xiii
Schorr, Lisbeth, xiii
Stretcher, V., 123

Taylor, Mark, xiii
TCC Group, 135–138
The California Endowment (TCE), 135–137
Thornley, Richard, xiii

U.S. Agency for International
   Development, 6
U.S. Department of Energy (DOE),
   110–112
   Energy Efficiency and Renewable
      Energy (EERE) programs,
      110–111
   Office of Planning, Budget, and
      Analysis, 110
U.S. Office of Juvenile Justice and
   Delinquency Prevention (OJJDP),
   126–127
U.S. Pathways Mapping Initiative
   (PMI), 128–130
   Ready for School and Succeeding at
      Third Grade map, 128–129
United Way of America, 6–7, 15,47

W. K. Kellogg Foundation, 7, 15, 128
Waddington, E., 103
Weiss, Carol, 6, 15, 32

York, Peter, xiii

Subject Index

Action, 55, 85
  maps, 5
  paths, 12, 14
Activities, 8, 12, 37, 39–45, 57, 59,
    76, 126, 127
  identifying, 44
  multiple, 42–43
  penetration, 10
  quality of, 10
  program, 101
  scope, 10, 41
  selecting, 51
  sequence, 10
Advocacy, policy, 135–138
Alignment, 82–83
Archetypes,
  definition of, 121
  examples of, 125–138
  exploring, 121–142
  value of, 124–125

Behavior change, 123–124

Causal loop diagrams
    (systems dynamics), 5, 92
Change effort recipe, 123–124
Community leadership development, 7–10
Critical thinking, 124–125

Data collection, 81–82

Effectiveness, 733
Evaluation, 50, 53–54, 82, 104–106,
    110–111, 116–117, 132
  as a navigational aid, 68
  design basics, 70–73, 114
  for effectiveness, 69–70
  formative, 69–70, 71, 86, 122
  framework for, 85, 122
  getting more out of, 67–70

literacy, 67–88
planning for, 68–69
quality, 84
questions, 10, 71, 74–77, 81, 84, 122
summative, 69, 71, 86, 122
system development, 117
Evidence based planning, 10

Feasibility, 50, 51, 52, 55–56, 85
  testing, 49
Feedback loops, 72
Frequency, 55, 78, 85

Graphic display, 89, 90, 98–117

Idea maps, 5, 17
Impact, 38, 40, 43, 51, 56–57, 59, 76,
    81, 92, 109
  progress towards, 115
Implementation fidelity/variance, 10
Indicators, 77–81
  and alignment, 82–83
  establishing, 10
  outcome, 78, 81
  process, 78, 79–80
Inputs, 96, 106
Intensity, 55, 78, 85
Intervention, 121, 127

Learning, 90–92
  "double loop," 73
  "single loop," 73
Logic, 51–52
Logic models
  benefits of, 3, 4–5, 91–92
  computer programs used in, 46
  creating, 3, 6, 91
  definition of, 3–5, 118
  development, 12
  effectiveness of, 12–13

evolution of, 6–7
features of, 6
improvement, 12, 49–63, 54
    generic, 129–134
    introducing, 3–15
    mark-up, 56–60
labeling, 10
program (PLM), 3, 5–6, 8–9, 12–14,
    35–48, 51–53, 59, 61, 73, 79, 85–86,
    90, 92–94, 114–115, 134
relationship of program and theory of
    change models, 35–39, 41, 46
shared, 45–46, 50
testing, 54–58, 60–61, 78, 80, 85
theory of change (TOC) logic models, 3,
    5–6, 9, 12, 13, 14, 18–32, 51, 61, 73,
    85, 86, 90, 92–94, 99, 113–114
uses, 3, 5–6, 72–73, 82–83, 91,
    99, 104–106
Logical frameworks (logframes), 5, 6, 92

Management, 67–68, 70
    programs, 101
Measurement, 43, 72, 80, 82, 117, 122
    connecting management and, 67–69
Mental models, 5
Modeling, 23, 49–63, 121
    and effectiveness, 50
    blind spots in, 31, 50–51
    myths, 50–51
    strand, 117

Organization theory, 104
Outcomes, 8, 14, 19–20, 37–38, 44, 80, 92,
    95, 99, 127, 132
    ambitious, 94
    "fair," 71
    groups, 104
    intermediate-term, 39, 40, 43, 45, 57, 76,
        97, 106, 126
    mandatory, 126
    long-term, 40, 43, 45, 59, 76, 80, 94,
        97–98, 106, 115, 116, 126
    short-term, 39, 40, 43, 45, 51, 57, 59, 76,
        80, 94, 96, 106, 126
Outputs, 8, 37, 39, 40, 45, 57, 59, 76, 79,
    101, 106, 115, 127
    mandatory, 126

Partnership, 101–102
    organization factors, 101
Performance standards, 83–84
Persuasion, 52–53
Plausibility, 51, 55, 85, 134

Priority areas, 115–116
Process streams, 93–95, 106
Program logic models (PLM), 3, 5–6,
    12–14, 51, 52–53, 61, 73, 85–86, 90,
    92–94, 114–115
    action steps for, 44–46
    activities, 43
    assumptions, 36, 38–39, 42, 134
    creating, 35–48, 53
    design, 8–9, 13
    definition of, 5–6
    dose, 38–39, 79
    elements of, 35–37
    effectiveness, hierarchy of, 6
    evaluation, 8–9, 13
    example, 8–9, 39
    features of, 6
    limitations of, 35
    health improvement, 40–44, 59
    nonlinear, 38
    strategies, 36, 41–43, 45

Quality,
    characteristics, 61
    questions, 58–60

Research, 22, 132
    strategies, 95–98
Resources, 37, 39, 40, 45, 51, 54,
    59, 60, 76, 115
    defining, 44
Results, *see* outcomes

Scale, 51–52
Specificity, 51–52, 55, 85
Strategy, 50, 51, 72, 94, 95, 96, 115, 121
    flagships and local, 94, 98
    leadership and engagement, 94, 98
    multiple, 20–21
    PLM, 36, 41–43, 45
    research, 95–98
    TOC, 19–20, 22, 23, 27, 29–32

Target audience, 55, 60, 78, 85, 103
Targeting outcomes of programs
    (top), 124
Testing, 54–56
    FIT, 55–58, 60, 61, 78, 85
    SMART, 55–58, 60, 61, 80, 85
Theory of change (TOC) logic models, 3,
    5–6, 12–14, 51, 61, 73, 85–86, 90,
    92–94, 99, 113–114
    application, 31–32
    assumptions brought to, 22–25

benchmarking, 24, 27
building and improving on, 17–33
creating, 8, 17–24, 23–24, 53
definition of, 5–6
evidence-based, 18–19
expanded, 93–94
features of, 6, 19, 9
health improvement, 21
improving, 24–31
multiple perspectives, 24–25
nonlinear, 28–29
plausible, 18–19

realistic, 21–22
results, 19–23, 27, 29–31
strategies, 19–20, 22, 23, 27, 29–32
success in, 25, 29–30
toggling, 24, 26, 27, 30–31
tough questions regarding, 30
Time frames, 51, 52, 60, 70–71

Utility, 50, 52–53

Variation, 89–92
Visual displays, 6

About the Authors

Lisa Wyatt Knowlton, EdD, received a BA in International Relations from Michigan State University, an MPA in International Relations from Western Michigan University, and an EdD in Management and Policy from Western Michigan University. Her work history includes extensive assignments in programming and management of private, community, and corporate philanthropy along with organizational development and government relations. She has managed many large change projects for the W. K. Kellogg Foundation along with special projects for the Aspen Institute, Bill and Melinda Gates Foundation, Independent Sector, Ball, Nokomis, and Kauffman Foundations. Lisa is a W. K. Kellogg National Leadership Fellow and has spent considerable time in Central America, Asia, and Europe. Her areas of specialization include strategy, team learning, organization development, leadership, change management, and systems thinking. She is a strategy architect, management guru, and learning coach with Phillips Wyatt Knowlton, Inc. She also speaks Spanish. You can reach her via e-mail at: lisawk@pwkinc.com. She lives in Battle Creek and Glenn, Michigan, with her husband, Tim, and daughter, Taylor.

Cynthia C. Phillips, PhD, received a BS in Biology and Chemistry from Indiana University, an MA in Educational Leadership from Western Michigan University, and a PhD in Measurement, Research & Evaluation from Western Michigan University. She has a rich work history that includes consultation with the W. K. Kellogg Foundation, Ball Foundation, Bill and Melinda Gates Foundation, Nokomis, Kauffman, and the David and Lucile Packard Foundations in the design and implementation of evaluation, evaluation training, and knowledge management projects. She is the author of the W. K. Kellogg Foundation *Logic Model Development Guide*. Cynthia is a sought-after presenter on logic models and knowledge management. Her areas of specialization and expertise include evaluation/measurement; knowledge management; organizational learning; logic models, quantitative methods, and qualitative methods; and electronic data collection and dissemination. Cynthia offers a user-friendly approach to evaluation capacity building. She is principal investigator, idea engineer, and measurement expert with Phillips Wyatt Knowlton, Inc. You can reach her via e-mail at: cynthiap@pwkinc.com. She lives in Richland, Michigan, with her husband, Dennis.

Phillips Wyatt Knowlton, Inc. is a measurement and management resource for systems and social change. It provides expert counsel in strategy, learning, and evaluation. For more information, see www.pwkinc.com.